God

FACETS

Selected Titles in the Facets Series

God
A Brief History

Paul E. Capetz

Fortress Press
Minneapolis

For George and Harriet

⌒

Cover image: Lance W. Clayton/Nønstock.

ISBN 0-8006-3630-9

The paper used in this publication meets the minimum
requirements of American National Standard for Infor-
mation Sciences – Permanence of Paper for Printed
Library Materials, ANSI Z329.48-1984.

Manufactured in the U.S.A.

07   06   05   04   03   1   2   3   4   5   6   7   8   9   10

Contents

Preface

This brief book invites the reader to survey the great sweep of two millennia of Christian reflection about God. It is an attempt at "historical theology." As a study in history, it follows a chronological framework for the sake of exploring how Christian understandings of God have developed from biblical times to the present day. As a study in theology, the narrative is designed to highlight some of the questions to be pondered by contemporary Christians as they consider how to articulate the meaning of faith in God for today. Since this discussion can only introduce the bare outlines of this history, there is no pretense to completeness in the treatment of topics. Indeed, specialized monographs have been written by learned scholars about every issue treated here in only a few sentences or paragraphs. Yet one can identify prominent lines of development and significant tensions within this extremely complex history. We can thereby arrive at some basic understanding of the affirmations about God made by Christians as well as the problems that have led to controversy among them about how to formulate these affirmations.

1

Judaism and the Development of Monotheism

The origins of Christian faith in God lie in the obscure prehistory of Israelite religion. Our primary source for reconstructing this history is the Jewish Bible, which is called the Old Testament by Christians. On account of the way the Old Testament was put together by its final editors, readers who begin with the creation story in Genesis and move on from there to the narratives about Adam and Eve, Noah, Abraham, Moses, David, and so on, receive the impression that Israel's faith had always been monotheistic. But modern critical study of the Bible has challenged this traditional viewpoint and has had to work against the grain of the final editors' version of the biblical story to piece together from its scattered clues how the religion of ancient Israel actually developed to the point when monotheism became the norm. It was only afterward that the previous history of Israel was then reinterpreted to give us the biblical story as we now have it.

Like other Near Eastern peoples, the Israelites assumed the reality of what we may call "deities" or "gods," that is, powerful beings who shape, for good or ill, the world in which human beings live. In general, we may say that the gods were personifications of the natural forces that create, sustain, and also sometimes threaten to destroy the necessary conditions for human life to flourish. Because the powers determining human life were imagined to be person-like, it was believed that the gods could be appeased by appropriate rituals. Performance of such rituals made up the core of ancient religions. The myths or stories about the gods indicated what these powers were like and explained the origin of the cosmos and the place of humanity within it.

The God Yahweh

Given the geographical location of Canaan (later to become "Israel") at the crossroads between Mesopotamia (Abraham's homeland) and Egypt (Moses' homeland), early Israelite religion and mythology originated within this matrix of cultures in the Fertile Crescent. Polytheism was characteristic of the world in which Israel was born. While Israel took for granted the reality of deities as did its neighbors, it rejected the worship of many gods and decided, instead, to worship only one deity. Still, this single-minded devotion to its own god was not yet monotheism. It was henotheism. Although the words *monotheism* and *henotheism* both refer to the worship of only one god, scholars employ these terms to make a distinction:

whereas the henotheist chooses to serve one god among many without denying the existence of other gods, the monotheist believes that there exists, in fact, only one true deity. The crucial question is how Israel eventually found its way to a full-fledged monotheistic theology, since this was the great turning point in its religious history apart from which neither Judaism nor Christianity would have come into being.

The twelve tribes that coalesced into a single nation were unified by their devotion to the god named Yahweh who had brought about their release from Egyptian servitude through his chosen instrument, Moses (Exod. 3:1-17). After the exodus, Moses exults: "Who is like you, O LORD [Yahweh], among the gods?" (Exod. 15:11).[1] Shortly thereafter, Yahweh placed Israel under obligation to worship him alone among the gods through the covenant sealed at Mount Sinai. The Ten Commandments given to Moses begin with Yahweh's introduction of himself as the deity that procured Israel's deliverance: "I am the LORD [Yahweh] your God, who brought you out of the land of Egypt, out of the house of slavery; you shall have no other gods before me" (Exod. 20:2-3). Israel is to be set apart as Yahweh's own special people. Yahweh then spells out the other religious and moral duties incumbent upon Israel in return for his favor. In Christian terms, the "law" is set within the context of the "gospel," that is, Israel's service to Yahweh is based upon gratitude for his provision of salvation. The exodus story thus provides the proper context for interpreting the legal materials in the Torah.

Israelite faith in Yahweh had some other peculiar characteristics as well. The first is the prohibition against making graven images or "idols" (Exod. 20:4; cf. Exod. 32). Related to this is the belief that Yahweh is invisible: "no one shall see me and live" (Exod. 33:20; cf. Isa. 6:5 and John 1:18a). Visual depiction of the gods and goddesses was common in the ancient world. Centuries later when foreign invaders entered the temple in Jerusalem, they were surprised to find that the Jews had no statue depicting their god. Instead, Yahweh made himself known to Israel through his words and deeds. Central to Israelite faith was the belief that Yahweh has acted in history for the sake of Israel's well-being: first, through his rescue of the people from slavery in Egypt and, second, through his conquest of the land of Canaan, which he long ago promised to Israel's ancestors (Deut. 26:1-11). This notion that Yahweh is an actor on the stage of history played a critical role in the development of the Bible's distinctive affirmations about God. Unlike the Canaanite deities, who were worshiped primarily to secure their powers of fertility to sustain agriculture and, as such, were believed to be manifested in the cyclical processes of nature, Yahweh was worshiped for his political power of breaking the bonds of injustice and oppression through his liberation of a powerless people. History, not nature, was Yahweh's primary domain; and thus political metaphors, such as king, lawgiver, warrior, ruler, or judge, play a prominent role in biblical descriptions of him.

After the conquest of Canaan under Joshua, the major temptation that beset Israel was syncretism: worshiping the gods of the indigenous Canaanites alongside Yahweh. No doubt, the new necessities of farming the land lent credibility to the view that it was prudent to appease gods who had a reputation for ensuring fertility. The prophets denounced this syncretism as a breach of fidelity to the covenant that Yahweh had made with Israel during its sojourn in the wilderness. The contest on Mount Carmel between the prophet Elijah and the representatives of the Canaanite god Baal is a classic illustration of this polemic against syncretism on behalf of a pure Yahwism: "How long will you go limping with two different opinions? If the LORD [Yahweh] is God, follow him; but if Baal, then follow him" (1 Kings 18:21).

During the tenth century B.C.E., the earlier tribal confederacy was replaced by a monarchy, first under Saul and then under David. This shift held great religious import since the institution of the monarchy was seen by conservative elements as a challenge to Yahweh's sole kingship over his people (1 Sam. 8:5-8; 12:12). Nonetheless, once the innovation of kingship was accepted, the Israelites became a nation-state like the other ancient Near Eastern peoples around them. The Davidic line was legitimated theologically by the belief that Yahweh had made a perpetual covenant with David to establish his throne forever (2 Sam. 7:11-16). David's son Solomon built a temple for Yahweh in Jerusalem (Zion), the nation's new capital. This, too, was an innovation; hitherto, Yahweh had always been "on the move," so to speak; his invisible presence was represented by the portable ark of the covenant (Exod. 25:10-22; 1 Chron. 17:4-6). Now Yahweh had his permanent dwelling in Jerusalem where his worship was centralized (2 Sam. 7:5-7; 1 Kings 8:27-30). When the ark containing the Decalogue was brought into the Temple, the act symbolized the effort to unite the Sinai tradition of Moses with the new Zion theology of David (1 Kings 8:1-21). But the united monarchy did not last long. By the end of the century there were two kingdoms, Israel in the north with its capital at Samaria and Judah in the south with its capital in Jerusalem. Israel was later defeated by Assyria in 722/21 B.C.E. After the Babylonians conquered Judah in 597/96 B.C.E., the chief political and religious leaders were deported to exile in Babylon. A decade later, the Temple itself was destroyed. The exile called into question the theological foundations of Yahwism.

The Defeat of Yahweh?

The collapse of the monarchy, the loss of the Temple, and the removal from the land all indicated the apparent defeat of Yahweh himself by the stronger gods of Babylon (Ps. 137:4). But the prophets had an answer to this dilemma and thereby pointed the way into the future. They interpreted the national crisis as Yahweh's punishment of his chosen people for their infidelity to the covenant. The exile signaled not a defeat for Yahweh but, rather, the vindication of his justice in upholding the terms of the

Mosaic covenant set forth in the Torah itself (Deut. 30:15-20). In response to the exilic crisis, the final version of the Torah (Pentateuch) was edited so that the sacred story of Israel now ends with Moses' instructions to the people in the wilderness as they are about to cross the Jordan river into the promised land. The significance of this new ending is to suggest that Israel in exile can still be God's people; fidelity to the covenant, not possession of the land, defines Israel's relation to God.[2] Moreover, that Yahweh could use Babylon to punish his chosen people suggested a broader view of his providential powers. Yahweh was now seen as the lord of all history, not just Israel's history.

This new interpretation of the national history thus reflected a profound change in the understanding of God. Previously, Yahweh had been the god of Israel; just as Egypt or Assyria had its gods, so Israel had Yahweh. But now he came to be seen as the only divine being, whereas the gods of the other nations were viewed as nonexistent; indeed, they were even held up to ridicule as mere figments of the imagination (Isa. 44:9-20). Yahweh was affirmed to be the sole deity because he created the world (Jer. 10:1-16). The creation narrative in the first chapter of Genesis, with which the Torah begins, also stems from this period. Here we witness for the first time an unambiguous expression of a thoroughgoing monotheism, in contrast to the earlier henotheism. From now on, God in the true sense is defined by his identity as creator of the world (Gen. 1:1). Whatever is not God belongs in the category of "the world." Hence, in monotheism, a clear line is drawn between the creator and the creation. Idolatry now came to mean worship of beings that are not truly divine because they are creatures. This was contrasted with worship of the one God who created the world.

With its identification of God as not only the savior who acts in history but also as the creator of the entire realm of nature, monotheism moved decisively beyond the confines of the earlier henotheistic theology. The divine power that saves was affirmed to be the same as that which creates. For the monotheist, the god of henotheism is a partial god, not the universal deity whose reign is coextensive with the world as a whole. Israel's deity was no longer just a tribal or national god; he was believed to be the one God of all nations whose sovereign lordship over history is grounded in his identity as creator of the world. Monotheism is thus the indispensable presupposition of the new faith of Judaism that emerged out of the ashes of henotheistic Yahwism.

On account of its belief in God as the creator of all things, monotheism implies a critique of polytheism, wherein the gods are personifications of the natural powers. By contrast, a monotheist views the powers of nature (such as harvest, reproduction, and the moon and the stars) as lacking divinity since they are part of God's creation; nature is the order designed by God. For this reason, these powers are not to be worshiped. Still, the affirmation that God is the creator, sustainer, and providential orderer of the natural world and not simply the lord of history indicates that the real existential problem represented by pre-exilic Israel's temptation to worship the Canaanite gods of nature had at last been adequately addressed. The lives of human beings are not determined solely by historical events, however redemptive they may be in liberating a people from oppression or establishing justice. Natural powers, such as those providing for a good harvest or freedom from disease, also impinge upon the quality of human life. The "wisdom" tradition in Israel gave expression to the theological implications of monotheism's affirmation that God is the ultimate power at work in and through the natural processes of life. In this tradition, God's ways are discerned by observation of the order evident in the world. The wise person is able to discern what God requires and to live in appropriate relation to God's world, which includes proper use and enjoyment of the blessings of the natural world such as food, wine, sexual love, and material goods. Indeed, the wisdom theology has almost a secular feel to it in that God's will is known through reflection upon common human experiences. Such knowledge is not sanctioned by appeal to the history of salvation.

After Babylon was defeated by Persia, the Persian ruler Cyrus issued an edict in 538 B.C.E. allowing the exiles to return to their homeland and to rebuild their temple. But not all Jews returned; many lived in Babylon and elsewhere. A new institution called the synagogue (assembly) arose where

Jews met for instruction in the Torah and praise of God. This became the central organization of Jewish religious life in the Diaspora since every city where Jews lived could have its own synagogue and one did not need to be in Jerusalem to worship God. During the exile, what we now call "Judaism" (the religion of the people of Judah) had begun to take on those distinctive traits (for example, circumcision, resting on the Sabbath, and observance of dietary regulations) designed to keep the Jews from the pollutions of idolaters. Nonetheless, in keeping with the transformation of its theology from henotheism to monotheism, Israel came to a new understanding of its election as God's chosen people. While intent upon remaining separate (or "holy"), the Jews saw themselves as entrusted with a mission to bear witness among the nations ("the Gentiles") to the one true God. Henceforth, Israel would live within the poles of its universal monotheism and its particularity as a separate people among the Gentiles.

2

Hellenism and the Emergence of Christianity

A new era began when Alexander the Great (356–323 B.C.E.) conquered most of the then-known world and brought it under the sway of Greek civilization. Out of the interaction between Greek culture and the various local cultures conquered by Alexander's armies, a new universal civilization called Hellenism (from the Greek word for Greece, *Hellas*) was born. The encounter of Judaism with Hellenism offered opportunities for the mutual enrichment of both cultures; at the same time, it generated serious tensions within Judaism itself regarding the most appropriate attitude for the Jews to adopt toward Hellenism. The Greeks considered themselves to possess a superior culture and made a sharp distinction between themselves and non-Greeks, whom they called "barbarians." Alexander aimed to bring "civilization" to the barbarians, including the Jews. For their part, the Jews were hoping to convert the Gentiles to the recognition of the one true God worshiped in Jerusalem (Ps. 117:1; Isa. 2:1-4; 56:6-8; Mal. 1:11). The fact that the New Testament was written in Greek is indicative of this confluence of Judaism and Hellenism (Rom. 1:14; 10:12; Gal. 3:28a).

Jewish Encounters with Hellenism

Some Jews embraced Hellenism selectively, adopting and adapting those parts of it deemed compatible with Jewish faith. Philo of Alexandria (ca. 20 B.C.E.–40 C.E.) provides a good example of a serious intellectual engagement with Greek philosophy on the part of an educated Jew. He had the dual purpose of enriching Judaism through the use of philosophical concepts and of explaining Judaism to Gentiles by means of these same conceptual resources. It was philosophy more than anything else in Greek culture that provided Philo and other like-minded Jewish thinkers with the most obvious point of contact between the traditions of Israel and Greece. The reason philosophy was of such great interest to Philo and others had to do with the criticism of polytheistic religion given by the Greek philosophers themselves.

Socrates (469–399 B.C.E.) marked the great turning point in the history of Greek philosophy. He was concerned to provide the Greek city-state with an ethical foundation based on reason. While a critique of polytheism had not been the direct object of his philosophical inquiries, it was to be expected that, like everything else, religious practice and belief would also be subjected to the rigor of his questioning. When this did happen, the myths were shown to be filled with contradictions; moreover, the gods were criticized for their immoral behaviors as depicted in the myths. The point scored by

Socrates was that the inherited stories about the gods narrated by Homer and the other poets could hardly serve the purpose of providing the necessary moral guidance for living a virtuous life. The goal of the Socratic pedagogy was to lead a life of virtue founded upon the rational "knowledge" of what is good, true, and beautiful (cf. Rom. 12:2; Phil. 4:8); thus, one consequence of this philosophical scrutiny was the conclusion that the traditional religious beliefs were based on nothing more than mere "opinion." While it is not clear whether Socrates himself actually denied the existence of the gods altogether, it is apparent that his critique did a great deal to undermine faith in the inherited traditions of polytheistic religion, at least on the part of intellectuals in his society.[1] Socrates was eventually sentenced to death by his fellow Athenians on the charge of atheism.

From the perspective of a Jew like Philo, the amazing fact that the philosophers engaged in this criticism of their own polytheistic traditions pointed the way toward a possible convergence between Greek philosophy and Jewish religion. Seizing upon this possibility, Philo sought to demonstrate that Judaism was, in fact, the "rational religion" sought by the philosophers (cf. Rom. 12:1).[2] Nonetheless, Philo knew there were aspects of the biblical depiction of God that were unacceptable to a philosophical mind. Just as the philosophers had been critical of the Greek deities when they were said to have acted irrationally and immorally, so, too, there were stories in the Bible in which Israel's God appeared to be vulnerable to the same charge. But the philosophers resolved this problem through the method of "allegorical" interpretation of the myths. An *allegory* is a story with a deeper, spiritual meaning than that which lies on the surface of the literal narrative (Gal. 4:24). As a result, philosophers could claim that the myths should not be taken literally since their real meaning is symbolic of philosophical truths. In this way, one did not need to reject the inherited religious traditions altogether since the allegorical method provided the means to reinterpret their meaning and truth. Philo embraced this method and applied it to the problematic texts in the Jewish scriptures. When read through this lens, the Bible was a philosophical text teaching monotheism and a rational code of ethics. This method of reading scripture became very influential in classical Christianity, and it enabled Augustine to move beyond his initial aversion to the Old Testament as barbaric and unworthy of a philosophical approach to religion.[3]

But Hellenism also posed a threat to the integrity of Jewish religion since it was difficult to participate in Greek culture (athletics, drama) without paying homage to the Greek gods. Indeed, some Jews were willing to give up the distinctive marks of Judaism in order to become fully Hellenized (2 Macc. 4:7-17). For non-Greek polytheists, of course, this was not a problem since one could worship the gods of Greece by identifying them with the gods worshiped in Rome or Egypt. But for Jewish monotheists, such syncretism was not possible.

The conflict with Hellenism became brutally clear when the temple was desecrated by the Seleucid (Syrian) ruler Antiochus IV Epiphanes in 168/67 B.C.E. In an attempt to enforce Hellenism, he turned the temple into a shrine dedicated to Yahweh, Baal, and Zeus (1 Macc. 1:41-64; 2 Macc. 6:1-11).

The Apocalyptic Impulse

During this era there arose a new impulse in Judaism called apocalypticism, which took a dim view of all Gentiles as idolaters and consequently rejected every effort at a rapprochement between Greek civilization and Jewish religion. An *apocalypse* is a revelation or disclosure of God's secret plan for history, which has been entrusted to ancient seers (cf. 1 Cor. 2:7). In this theology, the epochs of history are predetermined to become increasingly evil until such time as God intervenes to crush the dominion of evil in the world. The Book of Daniel, written in the second century B.C.E., is an example of this type of literature. Apocalyptic theology addresses the questions of *eschatology,* that is, the events expected to accompany the end of history. Apocalyptic Jews understood themselves to be living in the end-time and were awaiting God's messiah (Hebrew: "anointed"), who would be a king like David (2 Sam. 23:1; cf. Luke 1:32-33). While there were multiple conceptions of the messiah, all agreed that he was expected to overthrow the idolatrous Gentiles, to restore Israel to its former glory, and to purify the temple. Apocalypticism waits for this triumphant day when God's enemies are decisively defeated and God truly rules as king over Israel and the entire world. Hence, the end of history as we know it will bring about "the kingdom of God." Until then, the present evil age is ruled by Satan and his soldiers (the demons). Satan ("the adversary") is a new figure in Jewish theology who appears for the first time in the Book of Job where he is not God's enemy but rather God's agent for testing to see if the righteous Job will remain faithful to God under the stress of affliction. In apocalyptic theology, however, Satan is an angel who revolted against God and strives to usurp God's sovereignty over creation (Matt. 4:8-10). Although God is rightfully lord over the world, Satan is in fact wreaking havoc by creating conditions wherein it is almost impossible for Israel to live in fidelity to its covenant. And God allows this but only up to a point: when Satan is defeated, God's rule will be evident to all.

What is striking is the dualistic motif that has entered Judaism as a result of this new theological development. It is possible that this dualistic element entered Judaism as a result of its contact with the dualistic Persian religion called Zoroastrianism. Be that as it may, apocalyptic dualism is of a peculiar sort: it is a temporal or historical dualism, not a metaphysical dualism. Apocalypticism distinguished between two ages: this evil age and the kingdom of God to come shortly. This suggests that there had been a crisis in the monotheistic theology that emerged out of the prophetic movement to explain the exile. In the monotheistic view, this world is good because God created it (Gen. 1:31a).

Evil is accounted for as a result of human sin. Not only was the exile God's punishment for the nation's sin, but even disease afflicts individuals as God's judgment upon their infidelity (Ps. 6:1-2; Isa. 45:7; cf. John 9:1-3). History makes sense as the arena of responsible human action in relation to a just and sovereign deity. But apocalypticism, by contrast, gave expression to a deep doubt about the adequacy of this theological presupposition.

Unlike the prophets, the apocalyptic visionaries were not looking for a new redemptive act of God *within* history, such as the restoration under Cyrus. Instead, they were hoping that God would bring about the end of history; they envisioned redemption *from* history.[4] While some scholars believe that the prophetic movement itself gave rise to apocalyptic theology, it is clear that the locus of attention has shifted from history as the realm of God's redemptive acts (salvation history) to preoccupation with creation ("What kind of world is this?") and even to the ardent expectation of a "new creation" since this old one is completely under the sway of demonic forces (2 Cor. 5:17). The apostle Paul, Jewish monotheist though he is, can nonetheless speak of Satan as "the god of this world" (2 Cor. 4:4). What is problematic here is that dualistic motifs have been combined with monotheism, which is radically nondualistic. This created a deep tension within apocalyptic theology, which went as far in the direction of dualism as possible without actually abandoning the belief that the world was created by God.

Apocalypticism pointed to a real problem in the older tradition: it *is* difficult, in the final analysis, to explain evil within the framework of a consistent monotheism. The dilemma of Job clearly illustrates this. When Job protests his innocence and demands his day in court so as to vindicate himself before a just God, he is overwhelmed by the majesty and complexity of God's creation. God does vindicate Job's righteousness against those so-called friends of his who argue that Job must be guilty of something or else he would not be afflicted in these ways. But the point is that God designed the world in such a way as to transcend the capacities of human reason to understand it fully. We may indeed continue to trust in God's goodness and righteousness, but the ways of God are beyond human comprehension (Job 9:32-33; 38:1–42:6). The books of Job and Ecclesiastes are examples from the wisdom tradition in Israel indicating that the older assumptions no longer work (Eccles. 3:11; 7:15; 8:16-17). The prominence of the motif of creation in apocalyptic theologies has led to speculation as to the role played by Israel's wisdom tradition in this new development within Judaism. Whatever explanations historians give to account for apocalypticism, its challenge to the earlier biblical traditions of both prophecy and wisdom is clear.

There is one other important aspect to apocalyptic theology that needs to be mentioned: the belief in the final judgment and the resurrection of the dead. There isn't much mention in the Old Testament of life after death. Such references as one finds are to some vague sort of afterlife called Sheol. But this is really only a way of speaking of the realm of the dead and, in the earlier stages of Israelite and Jewish faith, there was no explicit affirmation of individual survival beyond the grave (Ps. 6:4-5; Eccles. 9:5-6; 12:7). Only in the later apocalyptic theology do we witness the emergence of this belief; the sole clear reference to it is found in Daniel 12:2. The idea that God will reward the faithful and punish the wicked after death follows from the abandonment of the belief that the righteous are rewarded in this life for their good deeds, just as the wicked are punished here on earth (Eccles. 7:15-16).

Jesus and His Followers

The proclamation of Jesus is to be understood against this background. Unfortunately, historians cannot reconstruct his teaching with great precision. The problem arises from the nature of the sources themselves: the writers of the four Gospels in the New Testament present Jesus' message through the lens of later Christian interpretation of his saving significance as the long-awaited messiah or Christ (Greek for "anointed one"). The "Jesus of history" and the "Christ of faith" are thus tightly interwoven in the narratives of the evangelists. Yet in spite of these historical problems, a few things can be said with relative assurance about the general character and tenor of Jesus' ministry, even if many of the details must elude clear focus.

Jesus gathered a following around his proclamation of what the evangelist Mark characterized as "the gospel [good news] of God": "The time is fulfilled, and the kingdom of God is at hand; repent, and believe in the gospel" (Mark 1:14-15). Like John the Baptist before him, Jesus announced the near arrival of God's kingdom or reign. Unlike John, who lived as an ascetic and warned sinners of the "the wrath to come" (Matt. 3:1-12), Jesus eschewed an ascetic lifestyle (Mark 2:18; Luke 5:33; cf. Matt. 6:16-18) and announced the coming of God's reign as a piece of joyful news (Luke 4:16-21). He called twelve disciples around him to signify the restoration of the twelve tribes of Israel. When he traveled to Jerusalem, he was hailed by his followers as the Son of David (Matt. 21:9). Once there, he staged a demonstration in the temple to protest its corruption. He even made a point of associating with "sinners," that is, those who were neither ritually nor morally pure, in order to gather them back into the fold of God's people, Israel (Mark 2:15-17; cf. Luke 7:34; 15:1-2). Indeed, Jesus believed his own work to be an anticipation of the kingdom since God's power was palpable in his words and deeds. In his healings and exorcisms, especially, Jesus saw that the power of Satan was at long last being overthrown (Mark 3:10-11, 14-15, 21-27; Luke 4:36). Luke depicts Jesus as making his inaugural address by citing the prophet Isaiah and proclaiming that now is the time when the prophecy is being fulfilled:

> The Spirit of the Lord is upon me, because he has anointed me to preach good news to the poor. He has sent me to proclaim release to the captives

and recovering of sight to the blind, to set at liberty those who are oppressed, to proclaim the acceptable year of the Lord. (Luke 4:18-19, citing Isa. 61:1-2)

Jesus was a Jewish teacher whose dominant devotion was living for the kingdom of God here and now, trusting that God's reign was already, in some sense, a present as well as a future reality (Luke 17:21; Matt. 6:10).

While the imminent advent of God's kingdom was the central motif of his preaching, Jesus also drew upon the other aspects of the biblical tradition to delineate his understanding of who God is and what God requires. He expounded the Torah to explicate God's will and summarized its precepts in the twofold obligation to love God above all things and to love the neighbor as oneself (Matt. 22:35-40; Deut. 6:5; and Lev. 19:18b). As did the prophets before him, Jesus criticized forms of religious observance that neglected basic moral obligations to the poor and the needy (Mark 7:6-13; Matt. 23:23; 25:31-46). Like Israel's wisdom teachers, he discerned God's providential care for all creatures in the course of natural events (Matt. 5:45; 6:25-34). Jesus' teaching about God was firmly rooted in the biblical-Jewish tradition even as he put his own distinctive stamp upon it.

The gospel proclaimed by Christians, however, is not the message *of* Jesus: rather, it is the good news *about* Jesus. The novelty of the Christian message emerged only after the Romans crucified Jesus as a claimant to be "king of the Jews" and his disciples testified that God had vindicated him by raising him from the dead (Rom. 1:4). They proclaimed that Jesus was Israel's long-awaited messiah, whose death had been a sacrifice for the atonement of sins but who would soon return in glory at the last day to establish the kingdom in power. With this message the "church" (from the Greek word *ekklesia* for "assembly") was born. Whereas Jesus had preached the nearness of God's sovereign reign when the forces of evil would be overthrown once and for all, the nascent church proclaimed his death and resurrection as God's decisive act inaugurating the turning of the ages.[5] This was an innovation in apocalyptic theology, which looked to the future, since the church now pointed to an event in the recent past, namely, Jesus' resurrection, as the sign that the kingdom of God had secured its definitive victory over Satan's rule. The "gospel" thus became the church's message about Jesus' significance in bringing salvation (compare the two uses of the word *gospel* in Mark 1:1 and 1:14-15).

Initially, what we now call Christianity was not a separate religion apart from Judaism; instead, it was a sect or movement within Judaism. Its distinctive belief was that the messiah has already come: he was Jesus who was crucified and then vindicated by God through his resurrection. The church understood itself to be the true remnant of Israel living in the interim between the messiah's first appearance in humility and his final coming (*parousia*) in glory in the not-too-distant future (Gal. 6:16; 1 Thess. 1:10; 4:13-18). Its missionary

zeal to evangelize fellow Jews grew out of its conviction that faith in Jesus would determine one's
standing before God on Judgment Day (Rom. 10:9-
10). But Judaism never anticipated a crucified messiah. The apostle Paul wrote of the proclamation of
the cross as "the power of God" and as "God's
weakness [that] is stronger than human strength."
Yet this same proclamation, he recognized, was "a
stumbling block to Jews" who "demand signs" of
messianic glory (1 Cor. 1:22-25). It was thus necessary for the church to reinterpret the prophecies so
that they could explain the phenomenon of a crucified messiah. According to Luke, this reinterpretation was initiated by the risen Jesus himself (Luke
24:13-35).

The church's eventual development from a Jewish sect to another religion alongside Judaism
came about through the mission to the Gentiles
and the emergence of Gentile Christianity in distinction from what is usually called "Jewish Christianity," though it would be better to call it
"Christian Judaism." The Gentile mission was one
expression of the hope for a new universal humanity that would transcend the distinctions between
Jew and Greek, civilized and barbarian, philosophers and nonphilosophers, men and women,
slaves and free persons (Gal. 3:28; Rom. 1:14; Col.
3:11). Conversion required of Gentiles a rejection of
polytheism (what Christians later called "pagan-
ism"). This aspect of the Christian mission was seen
as the fulfillment of the scriptural prophecies about
the conversion of the Gentiles from idolatry to the
worship of the one true God (1 Thess. 1:9). Many

Gentiles who had been exposed to the philosophical criticisms of pagan religion were sympathetic to Judaism. Such persons (the so-called God fearers) were among the prime targets of early Christian missionary activity (Acts 17:4, 17, and 18:7). Indeed, the synagogue and the church looked to them more like a philosophical school than a religion since there was no sacrifice in their services.

Whereas the ministry of Jesus was aimed at his fellow Jews, the ministry of Paul was aimed at the Gentiles. The genius of Paul lay in his combination of apocalyptic eschatology, on the one hand, with his willingness to speak in the religious and philosophical idioms of Greco-Roman culture, on the other. In Luke's history of the early church, Paul is depicted in Athens debating with representatives of the two most important philosophies of the day, Epicureanism and Stoicism. Luke even has Paul citing—with approval—religious affirmations made by pagan poets and philosophers: "In him [God] we live and move and have our being" and "we are indeed his [God's] offspring."[6] While Paul's criticism of superstition met with the approval of his Athenian listeners, his assertions about the resurrection were greeted with disbelief (Acts 17:16-34). Paul acknowledged that "Greeks seek wisdom" (*philosophy* means "love of wisdom"). Still, "the world did not know God through wisdom." Therefore, the gospel of the cross is "foolishness to Gentiles," though, in truth, it is "the wisdom of God" that is "wiser than human wisdom" (1 Cor. 1:21-25).

In Paul's own mind, the Gentiles should have served the one true God since whatever persons need to know about him is evident in the created order itself:

> For what can be known about God is plain to them, because God has shown it to them. Ever since the creation of the world his eternal power and divine nature, invisible though they are, have been understood and seen through the things he has made. So they are without excuse; for though they knew God, they did not honor him as God or give thanks to him, but they became futile in their thinking, and their senseless minds were darkened. Claiming to be wise, they became fools; and they exchanged the glory of the immortal God for images resembling a mortal human being or birds or animals or reptiles. (Rom. 1:19-23)

Paul's language here has roots in the "natural theology" of the Stoics. Natural theology reasons from the order of nature (*physis*) to affirmations about the reality and character of God. Natural theology is differentiated from "revealed" theology that bases itself upon a sacred text. If the knowledge of God has to be supernaturally revealed (in, for example, the Torah given to Moses on Sinai), then the idolatry of the Gentiles could be explained simply as resulting from their ignorance of this special revelation (Acts 17:30). But Paul insisted upon their guilt in suppressing the knowledge of God that all persons have by nature.

Paul claimed that Gentile immorality resulted from idolatry (Rom. 1:24-32). This view of the relation between Gentile religion and Gentile morality was typical among Jews (Wis. 14:27); but Paul's use of the terms *natural* and *unnatural* to describe, respectively, moral and immoral acts is another indication of his dependence upon the Stoics, who taught an ethics based on "natural law." In their view, true morality is taught by nature. This philosophical tradition of the natural moral law would become very influential in the subsequent development of Christian ethics, especially since Paul did not require Torah observance of Gentile converts to the gospel. Instead, he urged his Gentile converts to live according to the moral codes made popular by the Greco-Roman philosophers. Even the teachings of Jesus were not directly applicable to Gentiles insofar as Torah observance was the assumed framework of these teachings.[7]

This last point was a bone of contention between Paul and other leaders in the movement who insisted that Gentile converts embrace the Torah and live as Jews (Gal. 2). For these followers of Jesus, it was inconceivable that one could embrace the gospel without adopting Judaism since Jesus was, after all, proclaimed as Israel's messiah. How else does a non-Jew become a member of Israel except through conversion to Judaism? Paul argued that the Torah had been given to Israel as an interim measure until the coming of the messiah. God had promised Abraham that he would become the father of many nations. Abraham believed in God's promise and was "reckoned righteous" on account of his faith (Gen. 15:1-6). For Paul, the coming of Christ was the fulfillment of God's promise to Abraham (Rom. 4; Gal. 3:6-9). Paul noted that Abraham was justified by faith before having received circumcision. Hence, faith in God's promise, not circumcision, justifies. Between the time when the promise was made to Abraham and the time of its fulfillment in Christ, the Torah functioned like a guardian who oversees the minors until they reach their majority and become heirs of the promised inheritance (Gal. 3:23-26; 4:1-2). The gospel was preached beforehand to Abraham, so that all who have faith in the gospel are Abraham's children. Paul thus claimed that "a person is justified by faith apart from works of the law" (Rom. 3:28). Paul did not see himself as overturning the Torah since this is what he believed the scripture itself teaches (Rom. 3:31; Gal. 3:21-22). Yet he also saw this conclusion as entailed in the universality of biblical monotheism: "Or is God the God of Jews only? Is he not the God of Gentiles also? Yes, of Gentiles also, since God is one" (Rom. 3:29-30a). For those Jews in the churches who agreed with Paul, this teaching required a willingness to relinquish the customs and purity codes that had kept the Jews separated from non-Jews (see Acts 10; cf. Rom. 2:28-29 and 1 Cor. 9:19-23). Indeed, Paul gave an allegorical interpretation of the meanings of "Jew" and "circumcision": "He is a Jew who is one inwardly, and real circumcision is a matter of the heart, spiritual and not literal" (Rom. 2:29a). But other Christian Jews could not follow Paul here, and this created a split in the Jesus movement.

The other pivotal issue in the separation from Judaism was the direction of reflection upon the identity of Jesus in relation to God. It would eventuate in a doctrine of the Trinity. Many titles are applied to Jesus by the writers of the New Testament (for example, messiah, Son of David, Son of Man, Lord). Most controversial among these was perhaps Son of God, a term originally applied to the kings of Israel (2 Sam. 7:14; Ps. 2:7) and subsequently to the coming messiah. In keeping with the usage of the Old Testament, the language about Jesus as God's Son may originally have been honorific. The Gospels narrate that, at Jesus' baptism, God was heard to say, "This is my beloved son in whom I am well pleased" (Matt. 3:17). Jesus referred to God as his "father" (*abba* in Aramaic means something like "dearest father") and taught his disciples to call God "our father" (Matt. 6:9). Paul wrote that the baptized receive the Spirit, who makes it possible for them to pray to God as father, thereby being adopted into Jesus' relation of sonship with God (Rom. 8:14-17; Gal. 4:4-7). The early Christians viewed the outpouring of God's Spirit upon humanity as the fulfillment among them of an eschatological hope (Acts 2:1-21, citing Joel 2:28-29). "Spirit" had not yet been conceived as the "third person" of the Trinity. At this stage, the Spirit is the cause of miracles and other charismatic phenomena among Christians (Acts 8:14-24; 1 Cor. 12:1-11). More significantly, the Spirit is the divine power that breaks the bond of the demonic forces of sin and death so that the Christian who participates through baptism in the saving benefits of Christ's death and resurrection may be enabled to live in obedience to God (Gal. 5:16-26). In these statements we witness the beginnings of the distinctively Christian pattern in speaking about God. The relations between the three terms (God the Father, Jesus the Son, and the Holy Spirit) are not conceptually clarified by Paul or the other writers in the New Testament, though it is clear that the terms themselves were constitutive of Christian worship and theology from the very start.

In what is called a Christology "from below," Jesus was adopted by God as his Son either at the resurrection (Rom. 1:4) or at his baptism (Mark 1:9-11) or at his birth (Matt. 1:18-25; Luke 1:26-35). This type of "low" Christology was typical of the Jewish Christians who rejected the Christology "from above" that was normative in the Gentile church. In "high" Christology, Christ is conceived as a preexistent divine figure who assumed human form (Phil. 2:5-11; Col. 1:15-20). In the polytheistic context from which Gentile converts were drawn, it is hard to imagine that language about Jesus as God's Son was not interpreted by pagans through the lens of their mythology, which told of the gods and goddesses who had children of their own. In the second century, the apologist Athenagoras had to fight against this misunderstanding of what Christians meant by calling Jesus the Son of God.[8] If the incipient trinitarian language of Christians had to be differentiated from Gentile polytheism, it also had to be defended against the Jewish charge that it violated the basic premise of monotheism. In John's Gospel we read that the Jews accused Jesus of blasphemy because he made himself equal with God (John 5:18; 10:33; cf. Phil. 2:6), but we should understand this not as indicating what Jesus taught about himself but, rather, as reflecting what some Christians were teaching about him after his death. The problem for later Christian theology, which it will attempt to resolve with assistance from Greek philosophical categories, is how this high estimate of Jesus as God's Son can be reconciled with monotheism.

3
The Presuppositions of the Classical Christian Tradition

The need for greater clarity and precision in the use of Christian language about God and Jesus became apparent in the second-century church debates occasioned by the teachings of Marcion and the Gnostics. While their views were eventually rejected as heretical, they did push the emergent church to several decisions regarding the theological foundation on which the orthodox tradition would build its trinitarian theology. This foundation concerned nothing less than the monotheistic presupposition of the church's christological claims. The Gnostics and Marcion called into question whether Christianity is a monotheistic religion in basic continuity with Judaism. Although both heresies were dualistic, their reasons for advocating a dualistic theology were divergent.

The Dualistic Challenges

Marcion was motivated by soteriological concerns, that is, concerns about how humans are saved. Marcion's challenge to the church lay in his insistence that Christians repudiate the scriptural heritage of Judaism since the way of salvation taught in the old covenant is opposed to that offered in the new. This difference implied to Marcion that the Jewish religion was instigated by a different, inferior deity from the one whom Jesus revealed. The god known among Christians as the Father of Jesus Christ is not the same deity known by the Jews as Yahweh; while the Jews serve a god of law and justice, Christians are redeemed from his rule by a god of mercy and love. The identification of these two gods as one and the same was, in Marcion's view, the original heresy in the church that falsified the supposedly anti-Jewish message of Jesus. Marcion's theology is best understood as a radicalization of themes found in the letters of Paul, whom Marcion praised as the true defender of the gospel against its Judaizing distorters. Marcion was also the first to put together a canon or listing of New Testament scriptures. His canon contained the epistles of Paul and the Gospel of Luke, both of which he purged of what he believed were corrupt Jewish interpolations designed to soften the antithesis between Judaism and Christianity.

Unlike Marcion, who derived his dualism from considerations of salvation, the Gnostics developed a radical form of dualism that was heavily indebted to cosmological considerations. For them, the fundamental antithesis was metaphysical, that is, rooted in the ultimate structure of things. There are two ultimate principles of reality at war with one another: matter, which is evil, and spirit, which is

good. The god who sent Jesus is the spiritual principle, whereas the god who created the world is the
lesser material principle. Redemption is release
from this evil material world so that the scattered
divine sparks within human beings may be freed
from the prison of the body and reunited with their
divine spiritual source. To perform his redemptive
function in revealing the saving *gnosis* or knowledge that enlightens the human predicament, Jesus
could not have been truly a human being. Rather,
he merely appeared to be a person of flesh and
blood since otherwise he, too, would have been in
bondage to the material world from which he came
to deliver his Gnostic followers. It was necessary
for him to adopt the garb of humanity so as to
escape detection by the guardians keeping watch
over the prison of this world (cf. 1 Cor. 2:8). This
Christology is called *docetism* (meaning "to appear";
see 1 John 4:2; 2 John 7).

The origins of Gnosticism are still debated.
Some scholars have postulated that it represents
the extreme Hellenization of Christian doctrine.[1]
There is a certain plausibility to this view when one
understands the nature of Platonism, which exercised a profound influence upon Christian theology. Plato (ca. 429–347 B.C.E.), Socrates' greatest
pupil and founder of a school called the Academy,
developed a philosophical perspective on human
life in the world that bears a predisposition toward
dualistic thinking. Plato made a sharp distinction
between the rational soul, which is the divine element in us, and the material body with its irra-

tional passions. Virtue consists in disciplining the body's appetites and leading a life of reason. This same duality is reflected in his cosmology. The artificer of the world ("the demiurge") brought order into the disordered chaos of matter by imposing on it the eternal "Forms" or "Ideas," which served as a blueprint for the design of the cosmos.[2] Neither the physical body nor the material world is evil, according to Plato, but they are inferior to the rational soul and the changeless realm of the Forms, with which the rational soul has a natural affinity. One can imagine that it is a short step, indeed, from Platonism to Gnosticism, in which matter and the physical body are viewed as evil. Nevertheless, the hypothesis that Gnosticism arose through an excess of Greek influence upon the church assumes that Judaism and Hellenism are antithetical; hence, what is Jewish cannot be Hellenistic and vice-versa. But this fails to acknowledge just how deeply Hellenized various forms of Judaism actually were, not to mention how influential aspects of Judaism were on the Hellenistic mind.

Another possibility is that Gnosticism emerged after the utter disappointment of apocalyptic hopes. The Romans destroyed the second temple in 70 C.E. and defeated the Jews in their two rebellions against Rome (66-70, 132-35 C.E.). The messiah had not come to establish the kingdom of God. For Christians, the delay of Jesus' return in glory was a theological problem within the church around this time (2 Peter 3:3-4, 8-10). Perhaps Jews and Christians who had been hoping for a "new creation" were now tempted to oppose creation altogether and to turn their temporal dualism into a meta-physical one. In support of this thesis one may point to the many commentaries on the creation story in Genesis found among the Gnostic writings.[3] The Gnostic obsession with creation, then, would indicate the culmination of a trajectory that began with the wisdom tradition of Israel, in which God's ways were to be discerned through observation of the created world, through Job for whom God's creation was too mysterious to understand how evil might be explained, and then to the apocalyptic theologians who continued to believe that this world was originally God's good creation but that it had fallen under bondage to demonic forces. In any case, one can see just how problematic prophetic monotheism had become for many Jews and Christians. According to the prophetic theology, the deity who created the world and rules history is good and just. But history had not vindicated apocalyptic hopes and, as everyone knows, nature continues to be filled with sickness and death. However heretical Gnostic theology appeared, its answer was persuasive to many persons. This explanatory power has always been the strength of dualistic views over the apparent weakness of monotheism to account for evil.

The rejection of Marcion and the Gnostics was momentous for the subsequent development of Christian theology. Their challenge required the emerging orthodox church to determine the authentic "apostolic" tradition. This tradition included: (1) a canon of New Testament scriptures purported to have been authored—and thus author-ized—by the original apostles and their immediate followers, (2) a creedal statement or "rule of faith" (later to become the "Apostles' Creed") believed to reflect the common preaching of the apostles, and (3) an apostolic succession of bishops who have the authority to interpret the scriptures in accordance with the creed.[4] Also, the Christian canon included the Old Testament. This was not a mere editorial decision but a matter of great import since it secured the identity of the God who created the world and rules history with the God who redeems and renews persons through Jesus Christ. The des-ignation of the bipartite division of scripture as the "Old" and "New" Testaments is not a statement of antithetical principles of salvation; rather, it indicates the early church's conviction that differ-ent forms of the salvific activity of the one God move through the various stages of Israel's history until its consummation in the church (Jer. 31:31; 2 Cor. 3:15-16). Contra Marcion, the early church affirmed a fundamental continuity between Israel and the church. Moreover, the identity of the sav-ior with the creator entails that, contrary to the Gnostic rejection of the body and matter as evil, orthodoxy affirms the basic goodness of creation (Gen. 1:31). Matter is not evil, and the body is not the source of sin.

The all-important affirmation here is the Chris-tian doctrine that God created the world "out of nothing" (*creatio ex nihilo*). This means that there was no preexisting chaos or matter out of which God formed the world by imposing order upon it (as in dualistic views, such as Platonism). God created the matter or the "stuff" of the world as well. God is the sole metaphysical ultimate upon whom the world depends but who is in no way dependent upon it. This doctrine also implies that the Forms or Ideas of things are not external to God, as in Plato's view; rather, they are within the mind of God. Furthermore, the doctrine of creation is opposed to Stoic "pantheism" (from the Greek word *pan* meaning "all"), which equated God and the universe or nature as a whole; such a view does not preserve the necessary distinction between God and the world. Later, the Christian doctrine will have to be clarified in its relation to a monistic viewpoint such as neo-Platonism whereby the world is an "emanation" from God. Just as the classical Christian doctrine denies there is anything external to God which in any way conditions or resists him, so, too, it denies that creation is a necessity of his nature; rather, creation rests upon the free decision of God to create and exists in an asymmetrical relation of absolute dependence upon its creator.[5] This is what it means to affirm God's omnipotence: God is the ultimate power who freely bestows being on whatever exists. The Apostles' Creed begins: "I believe in God the Father Almighty, Maker of heaven and earth." Biblical scholars debate whether Gen.1:1 can appropriately be understood as teaching the doctrine of *creatio ex nihilo*; but it was so interpreted in classical Christian theology (see also 2 Macc. 7:28). Still, this doctrine does not claim to provide a metaphysical explanation of the origin of evil since it locates the source of evil in the human being and its sinfulness. The problem is not that the good soul is trapped in an evil material world; rather, the sinful soul relates itself inappropriately to the good material world created by God. Hence, redemption cannot mean release from the world; it can only mean restoration of the original possibility for right relationship with God.

The repudiation of all "docetic" tendencies in Christology was consistent with this basic affirmation of the goodness of the material world. It became crucial for the church to insist that Jesus was really born of a woman, that he lived and died under the conditions of human finitude (including his execution at a historically identifiable time and place), and that he rose bodily (Gal. 4:4; Phil. 2:8; see also the anti-docetic statements in the Apostles' Creed). Belief in the resurrection of the flesh signified that salvation is not of the soul apart from the body, as in views that postulate a preexistent soul temporarily inhabiting a mortal shell. Rather, God resurrects the entire person, body and soul. Eventually, the Jewish belief in resurrection will be harmonized with the Greek doctrine of the soul's immortality, but only with the qualification that God creates the human soul to be immortal and, therefore, the soul does not possess immortality in itself.

Forging the Doctrine of God

At the same time that orthodoxy began to assume definitive shape, Christians were appropriating the Greek philosophical legacy to defend Christianity against its detractors. Christians were persecuted as "atheists" in the Roman Empire because they refused to worship the gods of Rome. The Christian "apologists" (or defenders, such as Justin Martyr, d. ca. 165) were quick to see the parallel with the Athenians' charge against Socrates who had challenged Greek "superstition" by appealing to reason. The apologists get their name from the Greek word *apologia,* which means a reasoned defense of one's views, and this was the title of Plato's dialogue in which Socrates defends himself against the charge of atheism before the Athenians. In the New Testament, Christians are exhorted to "be ready to make your defense (*apologia*) to anyone who demands from you an accounting for the hope that is in you" (1 Peter 3:15). Hence, the apologists defended Christians as true philosophers who reject superstitious forms of worship (such as pagan sacrifice) and unworthy notions of deity through their embrace of a rational religion that teaches a virtuous lifestyle. By means of this argumentative and rhetorical strategy, the Christians sought to make the tradition of philosophy their own and to use its categories against the pagans. What we now speak of as the "classical" tradition of Christian theology began here. By lifting the concepts of the philosophers out of their original pagan context and fitting them to become the instruments for articulating the gospel in a persuasive fashion to the Romans, Christian theology forged that synthesis between biblical religion and Greek philosophy, which explains both its brilliance and many of its enduring tensions.

In their efforts to find a point of contact between philosophy and the gospel, the apologists continued the path opened up by such Jews as Philo. To be sure, not all Christians were happy about this attempt at a synthesis, just as many Jews had also rejected such an accommodation. Tertullian spoke for the antiphilosophical position when he asked: "What indeed has Athens to do with Jerusalem? What concord is there between the Academy and the Church?"[6] Even though the classical tradition would annex philosophy for its own purposes, there were good reasons for the hesitation expressed by Tertullian. The Hellenistic philosophical doctrines about deity had arisen from very different sorts of concerns and questions than those informing the biblical writers. Aside from Israel's wisdom tradition, which based its theological affirmations on observations from experience, the Bible's portrayal of God depends by and large upon the revelation of God in the saving acts of history. By contrast, the philosophers developed their ideas about the divine in the course of their speculations about the nature of being ("metaphysics"). They had been looking to find the ultimate explanatory principle that underlies all becoming. For the apologists, Israel's God was this metaphysical principle that is the cause of all things but is not caused by anything else (like Aristotle's "unmoved mover").[7] Yet the perennial challenge is whether one can truly identify the final principle of metaphysics with the biblical revelation of a personal God.[8]

While there were distinct schools of philosophy, they all tended to converge during the Hellenistic period. As a result most philosophers drew eclectically upon diverse sources for their doctrines. Such philosophical syncretism allows us to make generalizations about the common understanding of deity among the philosophers.[9] They had concluded from their cosmological considerations that the divine must be the origin of all, that it must be absolutely simple (not consisting of parts), and that it must be immutable, impassible, and timeless. These attributes are the "perfections" of God. For some philosophers, such as the neo-Platonists, God is also ineffable (beyond the capacity of the mind to know in a conceptual manner). The apologists adopted what appeared to be self-evident axioms derived from metaphysics and interpreted the biblical affirmations about God through these filters. But this synthesis made it difficult to understand how God could be a free personal agent who decides, judges, and loves, or, in other words, how God can be said to be truly related to the world. Indeed, the doctrine of God forged in the classical Christian tradition stood in some real tension with these aspects of the Bible.

In spite of these difficulties, the brilliance of this achievement lay in its ability to gain recognition for Christianity among many in the educated classes. Of particular importance in this respect was the apologists' use of the philosophical concept of the *logos* as a bridge between the gospel about Jesus and the tradition stemming from Socrates. *Logos* (from which we get our words "logic" and "logical") means "word," "thought," and "reason," and the term was employed by philosophers to refer to the principle of the divine self-manifestation in the world. The world is intelligible because it is the expression of the divine reason (*logos*), which can be understood by virtue of the participation of human reason (*logos*) in the rational structure of reality. With this concept, the apologists were able to explain how the philosophers could have known so much truth about God and embraced such a high moral code apart from biblical revelation. The *logos* concept was also identified by Christians as that which was fully embodied in Jesus. So, although the philosophers did not know the fullness of truth taught first by Israel and now by the church, they did catch glimpses of it on account of their inspiration by the divine reason.[10] In this way, the apologists baptized the tradition of philosophy, arguing that Christianity answered the rational questions of the Greek philosophers, just as it fulfilled the messianic expectations of Israel's prophets.

4

Christology and the Doctrine of the Trinity

A new era for the Christian church began in 324 C.E. when the emperor Constantine declared Christianity to be the official religion of the Roman Empire. As a result, the church's relation to its surrounding social and cultural world changed dramatically. Now no longer a persecuted apocalyptic sect awaiting the end of human history, it became a powerful institution that provided Roman society and culture with a new religious and moral foundation. For this reason, the historic creedal definitions of orthodox doctrine, developed during the fourth and fifth centuries, had more than merely theological significance; the political unity of the empire required a single statement of faith that was to be legally enforced. In "Christendom" heresy was prosecuted as a crime that undermined the religious foundation of society. Nonetheless, the theological issues at work in the formulation of the creeds were also vitally important as intellectual efforts to articulate the faith and must be understood as such.

Was Christ God?

The basic premise of the christological controversy is the statement in the Prologue to John's Gospel that Jesus is the *logos* incarnate. John wrote:

> In the beginning was the Word (*logos*) and the Word was with God, and the Word was God. He was in the beginning with God; all things were made through him, and without him was not anything made that was made. . . . And the Word became flesh (*sarx*) and dwelt among us, full of grace and truth; we have beheld his glory, glory as of the only Son from the Father. (John 1:1-3, 14)

The terms *Word* and *Son* are used to indicate Jesus' identity, so that he is both the Word of God and the Son of God. But it was the meaning of the *logos* in particular that generated the controversy leading to the Council of Nicea in 325. Specifically the question to be resolved was the relation of the divine in Christ (the Word) and God. John said that the Word was "with God" and "was God," but how can the *logos* be distinct from God and yet identical with God? On the surface, this looks polytheistic. But the monotheistic premise of orthodoxy, secured in the second-century struggles, precluded this possibility. So how are these affirmations to be rendered intelligible?

Arius (d. 336), an elder in the church of Alexandria, proposed an answer. He understood the *logos* as a creature made by God before God had begun to make the world and with whose help God subsequently created all other things. Arius drew this idea from another biblical text where "wisdom" (*sophia*) is personified as God's helper in creation:

> The LORD created me at the beginning of his work, the first of his acts of old. Ages ago I was set up, at the first, before the beginning of the earth. When there were no depths I was brought forth, when there were no springs abounding with water. Before the mountains had been shaped, before the hills, I was brought forth; before he had made the earth with its fields, or the first of the dust of the world. When he established the heavens, I was there, when he drew a circle on the face of the deep, when he made firm the skies above, when he established the fountains of the deep, when he assigned to the sea its limit, so that the waters might not transgress his command, when he marked out the foundations of the earth, then I was beside him, like a skilled worker. . . . (Prov. 8:22-30)

Arius identified the *sophia* of Proverbs with the *logos* of John. Recall that *logos* can also mean "reason," so John 1:1 could be translated, "In the beginning was Reason. . . ." For the philosophers, wisdom consisted in the pursuit of a life of reason; so the identification of the two terms was not arbitrary. The wisdom God used to create the world is the same as the divine reason through which "all things were made." Arius also inferred that the *logos* is a creature, which is what the Bible teaches about *sophia*.

Interpreting John 1 through the lens of Proverbs 8 enabled Arius to conclude that the Word is not divine as God is divine, since there is only one true God. The Word is a creature—an exalted creature, to be sure, since God had employed wisdom or reason in creating the world, but a creature nonetheless. On account of this special instrumental role as God's helper in creation, the Word received divinity as an honorific title, but this is not to be taken as a metaphysical attribute. For Arius, the strength of his position was that it preserved a strict monotheism while affirming Jesus' identity as the incarnation (embodiment) of the Word.

The problem with this formulation, as perceived by Athanasius (ca. 296–373), the bishop of Alexandria, was its implication that the church's worship of Jesus is idolatrous. Christians offered prayers to the risen Christ, who was believed to be present in the cultic gatherings of the church (Matt. 18:20; 28:17; Luke 24:29; John 20:28). If the Word or Son of God is not truly divine but only nominally so, this would subject the church's worship to the charge of idolatry, that is, of worshiping a creature. But there was also an important soteriological motive at work, for Athanasius denied that a creature, however exalted, could save fellow creatures from death. By his time, that had become the fundamental existential question to which the gospel was understood to provide an answer. According to Athanasius, while God made all creatures out of nothing, human beings were created in the rational image of God and, as such, were intended for immortality; but since Adam sinned, his progeny are subject to death (returning to the nothingness out of which creatures are made) as a just penalty for the fall from divine favor. The incarnation of the Word restored the divine image in humanity and bestowed immortality on Adam's children (Gen. 1:27; Col. 1:15a). To perform this salvific work, however, the Word cannot be a creature, made out of nothing, but must possess immortality by nature. To justify both the church's worship of Christ and the soteriology that the Word incarnate rescues human beings from mortality, Athanasius developed his understanding of the *logos* enshrined in the Nicene Creed.[1]

In the Nicene perspective, the Word is not a creature but is "true God from true God." This placed the *logos* squarely on the divine side of the creator-creation distinction. Moreover, the relation between God the Father and the Son (Word) of God is not that of the relation between God and the world: whereas creatures are "made" *ex nihilo*, the Son is "begotten, not made." This phrase is intended to specify that the relation between God and his Son is not that of creator to creature. Again, to make the point clearly, this statement denies that "once he [the Word] was not." Hence, the relation of the begotten Son to the Father is an eternal relation of which there was no beginning in the sense that creatures necessarily have a beginning. The crucial term, however, that was employed to distinguish the Athanasian view is *homoousion*, which means "of the same substance" or "of the same essence" (*ousia*). Although this word is not found in the New Testament, it became the technical metaphysical term marking out the orthodox doctrine, which the Arians could not affirm: the Word of God is not a creature but is fully divine in the same sense as God the Father is divine. For Athanasius, the full divinity of the Word secured the identity of the creator and the redeemer: "the renewal of creation has been wrought by the Self-same Word who made it in the beginning." [2] Thus the church's practice of worshiping Christ as divine became codified in its doctrine according to the principle, "the rule of prayer is the rule of doctrine" (*lex orandi, lex credendi*).

After the relation of the Son (or Word) to the Father had been worked out, it would take a while before there was an equally complete development of the doctrine of the Holy Spirit or "pneumatology" (from the Greek word for "breath" or "spirit," *pneuma*). At Nicea, it was merely affirmed: "and we believe in the Holy Spirit." This gives the impression of being almost an afterthought to the real locus of concern, which was Christology. But once it had been clarified that the Son is "of the same substance" with the Father, the understanding of the Holy Spirit as also being fully divine and co-eternal eventually fell into place of its own accord. The Constantinopolitan Creed of 381 affirmed that the Holy Spirit "proceeds from the Father, who is worshiped and glorified with the Father and the Son." This reflects the fuller development of reflection upon the Holy Spirit that had taken place in the interval since the Council of Nicea in 325.

How Is God Three?

But there was still the unresolved question whether this acknowledgment of divine plurality did not jeopardize the oneness of God, the affirmation of

which had been so central in the struggles against
Marcion and the Gnostics. Why make a distinction
within the deity between Father and Son and Spirit
at all? Why not simply explain that these differing
designations refer to the various modes of appre-
hending the one God in the history of salvation?
This was the question put by the representatives
of the "monarchian" or "modalist" tradition who
challenged the development of the *logos* theology.
These thinkers asserted that affirmation of the
divine unity entails the belief that God is a monad
or *monarchia* (meaning a "single principle"), which
is absolutely simple and without parts. The one
divine essence, however, can be said to express
itself in three operations or "modes" (hence, the
name "modalism"), but these distinctions do not
refer to anything real within the divine being itself.
Modalism thus tended to blur the distinctions
between Father, Son, and Spirit, leading its opponents to charge it with "patripassianism" (that is,
the doctrine that God the Father suffers). The argument goes like this: since (1) God is one and (2)
Christ is God incarnate, (3) it follows that God suffered during the incarnation. This view is also
called "Sabellianism," named after Sabellius, the
doctrine's best exponent in the third century. Even
though the Sabellian or modalist viewpoint safe-
guarded monotheism, it was rejected as heretical
on account of its implication that God is mutable
and passible as well as on account of its inability to
affirm the reality of the trinitarian distinctions
within the divine being.

The nonbiblical word *Trinity* (Latin: *trinitas*) was first introduced into the theological vocabulary of the church by Tertullian, who was suspicious of the influence of Greek philosophy upon the church's teaching. He opposed the patripassianism of the monarchians. There is a bit of irony in this, since he himself was quite influenced by Stoic materialism, and he even thought of the Spirit as being some sort of rarefied matter. Furthermore, the idea of the divine impassibility probably owed more to Greek philosophical assumptions about the divine nature than to the biblical heritage.[3] Nonetheless, in his opposition to monarchianism, he sought to articulate the real distinction of the persons. Anticipating the later doctrinal developments, he affirmed that God is one substance (*substantia*) involving three persons (*personae*). The term *person* did not yet signify the idea of an independent center of self-consciousness, as it does for us today. Tertullian's employment of the word is borrowed from the theater where it referred to the mask worn by an actor to play a specific character. The image suggests that one actor could play different roles. In Tertullian's view, God revealed himself in three different roles in the historical dispensation or "economy" of salvation. This is called an "economic" Trinity. In one sense, this view is not all that different from a certain form of modalism; but Tertullian really intended to indicate some real independence of the three persons in their "otherness" from one another.[4] The persons are distinguished according to "grade" or "aspect." Thus it is wrong to say that the Father suffered or was incarnate in Christ. Nonetheless, the unity of God is preserved by affirming that, while the distinctions are real, they are all expressions of a single divine power. Tertullian's introduction of this terminology was an important step in the direction of the full development of the orthodox doctrine of the Trinity.

If modalism appeared to swallow up the three persons in its concern with preserving the divine unity, the opposite extreme had to be avoided when emphasizing the distinct reality of the persons in their relation to one another. Whereas the Western or Latin tradition tended to a monarchian viewpoint, the Eastern or Greek tradition tended toward tritheism in its stress upon the independent subsistence of the three persons. The West began its reflections with the oneness of God and moved on from there to the puzzle of affirming the real distinction between the three persons. The East, on the other hand, began its reflections with the independent reality of the Father, Son, and Spirit and then found its characteristic difficulty in attempting to affirm the unity of God. These were the two extremes within which the church's trinitarianism had to find a mean.

The third-century theologian Origen illustrates well the dilemma of Greek theology. Heavily influenced by Platonic thought, Origen developed a pattern of reflection in which the divine plurality is conceived after the subordinationist model of a hierarchy of deities. In his system, only God the

Father is God in the strictest sense (*autótheos*), since he alone is unbegotten. The Son, though not a creature, is begotten and, hence, is a "secondary God" (*deúteros theós*).[5] The Son mediates between the Father and the realm of spiritual beings he has created, thereby serving as the bridge between the unity of God ("the One") and the multiplicity of souls he has made to be with him eternally ("the many"). The Holy Spirit is the highest being brought forth by the Father through his Son. There are thus three eternal divine persons (*hypostases*). Originally, the terms *hypostasis* and *ousia* were synonymous in meaning, both referring to "essence" or "being," but Origen tended to employ the former term in such manner as to connote individual subsistence or existence. For him, the three persons are one not in being (*ousia*) but solely by virtue of their unity in love. Hence, Origen taught a triad of divine beings that, though eternally co-existent, nonetheless stand in a hierarchical relation to one another. The Father is the source or fountainhead of deity, while the Son and the Spirit are subordinate to him in rank and dignity. But Origen's signal contribution was to suggest that the relations between the persons are eternal and not merely manifestations in the economy of revelation. Thereby, a significant step was made in the affirmation of what is called an "immanent Trinity."

The full resolution of the trinitarian problem was finally given in the fourth century by the Cappadocians: Basil, Gregory of Nazianzus, and Gregory of Nyssa. They taught that the three persons

exist eternally in three distinct modes of being
(*hypostases*) though sharing equally in one divine
nature (*ousia*). Thereby the real differences
between the persons are not glossed over, as in
modalism. Furthermore, the three persons are not
ranked according to their degrees of divinity, as in
a subordinationist model, even though the Cappadocians continued to maintain Origen's view
that the Father is the source or cause of divinity in
the Son and the Spirit. The Cappadocians thus
sought to avoid both a tritheism and a monarchian
interpretation of monotheism. They recognized,
however, that this confession of God as one nature
(Greek: *ousia*, Latin: *substantia*) in three persons
(Greek: *hypostases*, Latin: *personae*) is a mystery of
faith that cannot be rationally comprehended
by the finite human mind. Even though they
employed the analogy of a universal and its particular concrete expressions (for example, Peter and
Paul are individual persons sharing a common
human nature), they had to acknowledge the insuf-
ficiency of this example to convey the fullness of
meaning with respect to the one God who is yet a
Trinity. Later on, Augustine tried to find analogies
of the Trinity within the human soul, which is
made in the image of the triune God. In one version
he claimed that love exhibits a triune structure:
the lover, the beloved, and the power of love unit-
ing them; in another attempt, he spoke of memory,
understanding, and will as illustrating how God
can be three yet one.[6] However illuminating these
examples are, their proponents recognized the

limits to such analogies and, in the end, simply had to confess the inadequacy of capturing in human speech and thought the nature of the divine essence; as Gregory of Nyssa said, "We, following the suggestions of Scripture, have learned that the divine nature is unnameable and unutterable." [7] Still, their intention was to make an ontological or metaphysical affirmation about the divine reality in itself (*a se*), or in its "aseity" (the immanent Trinity), and not merely to state how it appears to us in the historical dispensation of salvation (the economic Trinity). The acceptance of the Cappadocian formula as the orthodox faith at the Council of Constantinople in 381 effectively put an end to the trinitarian controversy.

The Orthodox Position

At the same time that the church was attempting to work out its trinitarian doctrine of God, it was engaged in formulating with greater precision its christological doctrine. While the Nicene Creed—reaffirmed at Constantinople—had clarified the relation of the divine in Christ to the divinity of God the Father by means of its formula *homoousion* ("of the same substance"), what remained unclear was the relation of the fully divine Word or *logos* in Christ to Jesus' humanity. The central question was this: does the affirmation of Jesus Christ as "the Word incarnate" mean that Jesus had a real human mind as well as a real human body? Whereas Athanasius had clarified the nature of the divine in Christ, he left ambiguous the nature of the savior's humanity. John said that "the Word (*logos*) became flesh (*sarx*)." The genuine reality of Jesus' physical body had been important to orthodoxy ever since its polemic against the docetic Christology of the Gnostics. Though Athanasius never denied that *sarx* included a human mind in Jesus in addition to the divine mind (*logos*), he never affirmed it either. After much struggle this question was eventually resolved at the Council of Chalcedon in 451. The council affirmed that Jesus Christ is not only *homoousion* with God the Father with respect to his divine nature but also *homoousion* with us in his human nature (that is, he had both a real human body and a real human mind). The only difference between his humanity and ours is that he was without sin (Heb. 4:15b.). This long development culminated in the dual affirmations of orthodox Christian faith: (1) God is three persons in one nature and (2) the second person of the Trinity (the Word or Son of God) is both fully divine and fully human. The doctrines of the Trinity and Christology thus form an essential unity. These twin doctrines continue to serve as the doctrinal foundation for Eastern Orthodoxy, Roman Catholicism, and mainline Protestantism.

Since all the persons of the Trinity are fully divine, there is no hierarchical subordination of the relations of the persons to one another as though divinity were somehow a matter of degree. Hence, whatever is predicated of God as God is to be attributed to all three persons equally; since God is the creator, it follows that "uncreated" applies equally to the entire Trinity and not simply to the

Father. Distinctions are made, though, when an attribute is proper to only one of the persons by itself. The predicate "unbegotten" applies to God as Father but it cannot be said of the Son, who is "begotten" of the Father. Conversely, it cannot be said of the Father that he is "begotten."[8] "Procession" (or "spiration") is the technical term proper to the Holy Spirit, but not to the Father or the Son. Controversy arose, however, over the precise relations of the third person to the other two.

In the sixth century, the Latin version of the Nicene-Constantinopolitan Creed was amended through the insertion of the phrase "and the Son" (*filioque*) to describe the Holy Spirit's procession. This became a bone of contention between the East and the West. The Western version of the creed states that the Spirit "proceeds from the Father and the Son," whereas the more original Eastern version simply says that the Spirit "proceeds from the Father." Opponents of the *filioque* clause argued that it represents a fundamentally flawed understanding of the Trinity since the distinct integrity of the Holy Spirit is threatened through the complete subordination of pneumatology to Christology with the result that the doctrine taught is actually binitarian. Moreover, it implies that there are two divine sources of the Holy Spirit, thus imperiling the Father's unique status as the fountainhead of divinity in the Son and the Spirit. Proponents of the Western addition to the creed argued that the *filioque* clause properly insists upon the inseparable relation of Father and Son, so that there is no activity of the Spirit that is not a witness to Jesus Christ, who is the Son of the Father. This emphasis thus attempts to combat all forms of "enthusiasm" that might lead away from Christ in the name of the Holy Spirit.[9] This disagreement between the East and the West regarding the *filioque* clause has never been resolved and remains one of the major issues in ecumenical discussions.

Throughout the history of Christianity there have been divergent views as to whether the trinitarian doctrine makes sense in the light of its historical development. Judaism and Islam, the other two monotheistic traditions to which the legacy of ancient Israel gave rise, have equated trinitarianism with tritheism and thus have charged Christians with a denial of monotheistic faith. This was clearly not the intention of orthodoxy, which had to formulate its theology against the background of Greco-Roman polytheism. But the Christians were faced with a difficult problem in their efforts to articulate their conviction that the one God had become incarnate in Christ. So we bring this section to a close by posing three questions that remain open-ended issues. First, is the Christian doctrine of the Trinity a form of monotheism, a form of polytheism (tritheism), or is it something else that transcends the dichotomy of either monotheism or polytheism? Second, what role did Greek philosophy play in the development of this doctrine, and how should this be evaluated? And third, did the doctrine of the Trinity as we now have it emerge as a function or a by-product of the christological controversy surrounding the meaning of the *logos* and, furthermore, would it have developed as a theological doctrine about God if some other way of thinking about Christology had made itself normative? Although these questions cannot be answered here, they do point to future controversies about the status of this doctrine.

5

The Middle Ages

Augustine (354–430) provided the link between the ancient world and the medieval civilization of Western Europe, which developed in the aftermath of the collapse of the Roman Empire in 476. He is called "the man of many conversions." Early on he rejected the Christian faith of his mother and devoted himself to philosophy in pursuit of truth. Soon he became captivated by Manicheanism, a dualistic religion of Persian origin, much like Gnosticism. It seemed to offer him a rational explanation of evil in the world. Persistent questioning, however, eventually led to disillusionment with the vaunted rationality of Manichean theology and brought the young Augustine to embrace academic skepticism for a period. According to the skeptics, Socrates had not taught philosophy as a way of leading the mind to certainty; rather, his purpose was to demonstrate the uncertainty of every purported claim to knowledge, thus inculcating in the wise person a studied agnosticism about what is real and true. But skepticism is a difficult posture to sustain over the long haul, and Augustine could not remain satisfied with it. Ambrose (340–397), the bishop of Milan, introduced him to neo-Platonism. This was a mystical development of Platonic themes undertaken by Plotinus (205–270). After embracing neo-Platonism, Augustine was intellectually prepared for the dramatic conversion of his heart that led him back to the Catholic faith he had initially rejected.

The God of Augustine

Augustine made the case that knowledge of God is to be found through self-knowledge. Like Plato, he believed that truth cannot be known *a posteriori* through the senses; it can only be known by looking within. Self-knowledge, for Augustine, is not merely subjective since in the depths of the soul one encounters God. Hence he said that he wanted to know nothing more than the soul and God. In knowing God, one knows the truth by which other things are known. But Augustine departed from Plato's idea that our knowledge results from recollection of what the pre-existent soul had known prior to its assumption of a body. Augustine rejected this view; since there is no pre-existent soul, knowledge is to be explained as God's inner illumination of the mind. Skepticism is refuted on its own terms: even the skeptic who claims there is no truth at least believes that to be a true statement. If I admit to being in error, I concede both the truth of my own existence—since I must exist in order to err—and the reality of truth itself.[1] This grounding of truth through reflection upon the knowing subject anticipated Descartes's formulation of the basis for epistemological certainty: "I think, therefore I am."

Neo-Platonism assisted Augustine in his defense of the goodness of God's world in the face of Manichean dualism. Plotinus taught that all things ("the many") are emanations of a single ultimate principle ("the One") from which they proceed (*exitus*) and to which they are destined to return (*reditus*). Unlike a dualism, which posits two conflicting principles of reality, such as matter and spirit, this monism teaches that everything that is has a common source. Nonetheless, some things are closer to their source than others. Imagine someone throwing a pebble into a lake and the concentric circles moving away with decreasing intensity from the point of contact where the stone hits the water. While all things alike proceed from the same fountain of being and goodness, material things are farther away from it than are intelligible and spiritual realities, which thus bear a greater likeness to it. This is a hierarchical conception in which things can be placed higher or lower on the ladder of being. That which is lower ought to look upward to that which is higher so as to facilitate its return to the One.

From the neo-Platonists Augustine learned to conceive of the soul and God as spiritual substances, not as material, which is how many ancients viewed them.[2] The soul has a natural desire for happiness. God, being a spiritual reality, is the supreme end of the soul's happiness: "Our hearts are restless till they find their rest in Thee."[3] Evil does not stem from the material body and its passions. Evil is a result of sin; it is a disorder in the soul and the direction of its desires or loves. The ideal for human existence—as taught by Jesus in his summary of the law—is love or *caritas* (the Latin translation of the Greek *agape*): properly ordered love of God and God's world, including ourselves as part of the creation. Note that the ideal is not to love God and to despise the world! But it does mean that there are different forms of love appropriate to God and to the world. We are to love God with the love of enjoyment (as an end in himself), and to love the world with the love of use (as a means to the end of loving God). Sin is a sickness in the soul that has reversed the proper order of its loves, so that it now loves God with the love of use and loves the world with the love of enjoyment (*cupiditas*).[4] Hence creation is loved with the kind of love appropriate only to the creator. Whereas *caritas* draws the soul up to God, *cupiditas* draws it away from God. Augustine has formulated the problem of idolatry using the category of love.

For Augustine, although our relation to the world and its creator is disordered, there is nothing wrong with the world as such.[5] Moreover, evil is not a substance at all: it is not a something, but only a nothing. It is a privation or lack of an original good, much like a piece of spoiled fruit was once delectable; indeed, it cannot be said to have become spoiled without its having first been healthy. Evil is ontologically parasitic upon the good. To exist is itself a good. Hence the idea of an evil substance is a contradiction in terms, since whatever has being is good simply as such (*esse qua esse bonum est*). A corrupted good is still a good insofar as it exists at all. Sin is the corruption of a rational soul through the misuse of its freedom. The root of sin is pride: we refuse to accept our complete dependence upon God who is the infinitely good source of being; instead, we seek our ultimate happiness in the finite goods of the world created by God. This means that a rational explanation for evil is not possible; evil results from the irrational choice of sin.

Although neo-Platonic categories proved useful to Augustine, it is clear that his own thinking stood in some tension with the Platonic heritage. This is evident in his positive appreciation of time and history. For the Platonists, this temporal world of becoming is fallen from the eternal realm of being. Redemption is release from time and change. But, for Augustine, temporal existence is not evil; time is good.

God is eternal, not temporal. In creating the world, God created time itself; Augustine explains, "there can be no doubt that the world was not created *in* time but *with* time."[6] Hence time does not exist for God. Nor does eternity mean endless duration. It is absurd to ask what God was doing before God made the world! The six days of creation recounted in Genesis do not signify a process in time during which God was at work, since that would subject God to the temporal process. Yet when we try to grasp just what eternity does mean, the effort stretches our ability to comprehend: the best we can say is that past and future are simultaneously present to God.

God created time for our salvation. We are to use it to attain eternal happiness through union with God. Life is conceived as a pilgrimage to be lived by faith, hope, and love. At the end of our journey, faith and hope will disappear since we shall see God in whom we have believed and for whom we have hoped; only love will remain (1 Cor. 13:13). This is the "beatific vision," seeing God face to face, which alone will make us truly happy (Matt. 5:8).[7] Augustine's *Confessions* illustrate how God worked providentially through the contingent details of his biography to bring about his conversion. Such detailed attention to the concrete facts of an individual life through time is inconceivable for Plato or Plotinus! History itself is the tale of two cities built upon the two loves: there is the heavenly city based upon *caritas* and the earthly city based upon *cupiditas*.[8] Until the eschaton, these two cities will be in ceaseless struggle with one another. Augustine rejected the Greek idea of time as cyclical in favor of the biblical view that time has a goal or *telos*: the kingdom of God. History is meaningful because it is providentially ruled by God, not by uncaring fate or capricious chance.

Within history, the church remains a "mixed body" and is not to be identified unambiguously with the kingdom of God. On the last day, God will separate the wheat from the chaff (Matt. 13:24-30);

in the meantime, we are not to seek a pure church of the saints. Hence Augustine rejected the sectarian ecclesiology of the Donatists in favor of an inclusive church of sinners. The church is a hospital for those who are sick in soul and need healing; it is not a gymnasium for the healthy and the fit to exercise their virtues. Augustine viewed grace as a supernatural power which, like a spiritual medicine, heals the disease of sin through the sacramental "means of grace." The priest is the minister of Christ the physician who dispenses grace through the sacraments, quite apart from the priest's own subjective worthiness in a moral or spiritual sense. The sacraments thus have an "objective" validity *ex opere operato* ("from the work having been performed").

Another indication of Augustine's departure from Platonism is the emphasis he placed on the heart or the will. Unlike the conversion of the intellect called for by the philosophers, Augustine understood that real conversion has to take place in the heart through a reordering of its desires. And he moved even further away from Platonism when, later in his life, he spoke of the corruption of the mind itself by sin. Accordingly, even the intellect is not free of the heart's loves; if the heart is corrupted, the mind will interpret the world with a bias rooted in disordered affections. Such a view of human existence and the depth of its corruption by sin represents a significant departure from Platonic rationalism whereby "to know the good is to do the good." Hence faith becomes more important than knowledge, since God's grace is necessary to enable us to do the good. In this respect, Augustine's theology reflects a new engagement with the epistles of Paul; just as the *logos* Christology of John had set the terms for the formation of patristic theology, so Paul's wrestling with the meaning of faith, grace, and election provided the framework for Latin theology in the West. Augustine found in Paul a mirror of his own struggles with a recalcitrant will (Rom. 7:15-24). His development of Pauline themes earned him the title *doctor gratiae*, the teacher of grace.

Against the Manichees, Augustine had defended human freedom. In his debate with Pelagius (d. ca. 419), however, Augustine appeared to reverse himself by arguing for the will's bondage to evil and, hence, its lack of freedom. Pelagius affirmed that the will is free; therefore, it is possible for us to fulfill the law and to merit salvation. Indeed, the obligation to be virtuous presupposes the capacity to bring forth the good; as Kant later put it, "ought implies can." But Augustine insisted that, after the fall, the original freedom of the will no longer exists. In our fallen state we don't have the ability not to sin (*non posse non peccare*). Augustine's view of human existence is not individualistic but historical and collective: Adam's misuse of freedom has altered the possibilities for human existence on the part of his descendants, who all participate in his rebellion against God. This lack of freedom to fulfill our obligation entails the need for grace. For Augustine, grace means that God does for us what we cannot do for ourselves by giving us the new direction of our heart's desires. He cited Paul, who wrote, "God's love has been poured into our hearts through the Holy Spirit which has been given to us" (Rom. 5:5), there "God's love" is understood as an objective genitive; a new love *for* God on our part is introduced into the order of our affections by the transformative activity of the Spirit. The paradox in Augustine's theology is that he first appealed to the freedom of the will in order to explain evil as resulting from human sin, thereby exonerating God from responsibility for creating a flawed world; but he then denied the will's freedom in order to uphold the idea that salvation is a gift of grace alone (*sola gratia*).

The debate with Pelagius raised serious issues not only about the freedom of the human being but also about the justice of God. If we do not have the freedom not to sin, how can we be held account-able for sin? Both Pelagius and the Donatists understood sin as vice and grace as a growth in virtue. But in looking upon sin as, instead, a sick-ness of the soul and grace as a divine medicine, Augustine insisted that the problem is more serious and requires more drastic measures. After all, a sick person cannot simply decide to become healthy; the doctor has to prescribe a medicine that can work as a powerful antidote to the debilitating effects of the disease. But this raises another ques-tion: if salvation is by grace alone, who initiates the process of salvation: the human being or God? Although a sick person cannot choose to become healthy, it is still possible to call for a doctor. While we may need God's grace to heal our sin, doesn't the bestowal of grace depend upon our prior decision for faith in God's grace?

Early on in his controversy with Pelagius, Augustine affirmed that the *initium fidei* or the initiation of faith lies with us.[9] This position has come to be known as semi-Pelagianism since it leaves some room for human response in the fallen state. Upon further reflection, however, he came to the view that even faith itself is a gift of grace. This belief that God initiates the process of salvation implies a doctrine of predestination: God "elects" or chooses those who will receive grace apart from any consideration of merit on the part of the recipient (*ante praevisa merita*). Logically, this entailed a doctrine of "double predestination" whereby God divided the human race into two, the reprobate and the elect. To Pelagius, this doctrine made a mockery of God's justice and violated passages of scripture in which human ability to turn away from sin is presupposed and God's will for universal salvation is asserted (for example, Matt. 5:48; 1 Tim. 2:4). But Augustine averred that God's justice is displayed in the damnation of the reprobate while God's mercy is shown in his free election of some to salvation (Rom. 9:14-24). Just as he had earlier introduced an element of irrationality into his account of human existence in order to explain sin, so, too, he now emphasized the inscrutability of God's will in disposing of his creatures as it pleased him. For Augustine, God's omnipotence is not bound by any constraints and God's will is not comprehensible by human reason. Paradoxically, this monism of grace led to another form of dualistic determinism in the destinies of the elect and the reprobate.

Though the Catholic church in the West condemned Pelagianism as "works righteousness," it accepted Augustine's theology only with qualification. In 529 the Council of Orange embraced a moderate Augustinianism. It rejected Augustine's doctrine of double predestination in favor of a doctrine of single predestination: God elects those who are to be saved, while merely permitting the perdition of the reprobate. With this ambiguous legacy, the door was left open to still further debates within the Western tradition that looked upon Augustine as its great "teacher of grace."

Mysticism and the East

Augustine was influential only in the West. Eastern Orthodoxy never went through a Pelagian controversy, nor did it look upon Augustine as one of its own church fathers. Nonetheless, the christianizing of neo-Platonism was a concern in the East as well because of the popularity of the writings of Pseudo-Dionysius the Areopagite, so-named because of the fiction that he was Paul's convert in Athens (Acts 17:34). In point of fact, his work stems from the fifth or sixth century. Dionysius is the father of mystical theology. Theology in the mystical tradition aims to elevate the mind above the sensible and intelligible things of the world so as to facilitate the soul's return to God.

Dionysius insisted upon the symbolic (nonliteral) character of all our language about God ("the divine names"). He distinguished between a positive way of speaking about God (kataphatic theology, from the Greek word *kataphasis* meaning "affirmation") and a negative way of speaking about God (apophatic theology, from the word *apophasis* meaning "negation"). Positive statements about God can be misleading as, for example, when the Bible says that God is a shepherd (Ps. 23:1) or a fortress (Ps. 59:17). Their purpose is to shock us by their dissimilarity. Recognition of the failure of all our positive speech about God leads to the negative way or *via negativa*: saying what God is not. Since God is beyond the categories of finite thought, God cannot be grasped conceptually by the mind. He is not only "invisible" (Col. 1:15) but also "unsearchable" and "inscrutable" (Rom. 11:33b). Through a combination of kataphatic and apophatic moments, we can approach the limits of our understanding. For Dionysius, as for other neo-Platonists, God is beyond even the category of "being." Since God is the cause of existence, he cannot be a member of the class of existing things. Hence, it is wrong to call God a being or even to speak of him as the supreme being. But, while negation is more important than affirmation, even negation is, in the final analysis, inadequate. Dionysius thus calls God "supra-existent," since God actually surpasses the distinction between being and nonbeing.[10] Our best "knowledge" of God, then, is really a kind of ignorance: it consists in recognizing that we cannot know the divine essence.

The identification of "the One" of neo-Platonism with the God of Christian faith was not without its tensions. The problem posed by the mystical theology of Dionysius is that it appeared to conflict with the orthodox belief that God has made himself known in Christ's incarnation. Moreover, when the Bible speaks of God, it uses personal terms for the most part; but neo-Platonism transcends such personal language in its *via negativa*. Also, the idea that the world is an "emanation" from God raised the question whether a distinction between the creator and the creation can still be preserved using these categories. Does this monistic metaphysics lead to the pantheistic affirmation that all things are parts of God? And what becomes of a personal relation to God when the soul is thought to return to its source in the One that is beyond attributes? Does the soul lose its individuality through absorption into the One? In all fairness to Dionysius, it should be admitted that one could ask a similar question of his presumed mentor, the apostle Paul, who affirmed that, in the eschaton, God will be "all in all" (1 Cor. 15:28).[11] But in Paul's writings, this is not the dominant motif. In one respect, Dionysius was simply articulating the mystical spirituality of the Cappodocian fathers. In another respect, however, his development of these neo-Platonic themes threatened to swallow up the orthodox affirmation that God is knowable through Christ and the church.

Maximus the Confessor (ca. 580–662) saved the legacy of Dionysius for orthodoxy by supplying the necessary christological and trinitarian framework within which to appropriate his neo-Platonic mystical spirituality. The important motif here is that of "deification" (*theosis*): just as God became human in Christ, so Christ makes us divine. Through sacramental union with Christ, we become partakers in his divine nature (2 Peter 1:3-4). The church's liturgy is the proper locus for the mystical union with God, who is otherwise unknowable to the rational mind. Neo-Platonic mysticism was thus baptized and exercised a decisive influence upon medieval spirituality and theology.

Icons were particularly important in the East as expressions of this mystical theology, but they had to be defended against iconoclasts who claimed that the use of icons was idolatrous. John of Damascus (ca. 675–ca. 749), the last of the great Eastern fathers, was the articulate defender of icons and their importance in orthodox worship. The icon, John explained, does not portray Christ's divine nature—which would be idolatrous!—but only his human nature. Nonetheless, through representation of his human nature, the icon lifts up the mind to contemplation of his divine nature. Furthermore, to reject the icon is to despise matter, which is a Manichean attitude. The spiritual and invisible became material and visible in Christ. John made a crucial distinction between "veneration" (*proskinesis*) of an icon and "worship" (*latreia*) of God.[12] Thereby he saved icons for use in the liturgy since the veneration of the icon does not violate the biblical prohibition against worshiping graven images (Exod. 20:4-5a).

Reason and Revelation

A very different approach to the knowledge of God than that found in the mystical tradition was undertaken by the scholastic theologians in the West. "Scholasticism" (from the Latin word *schola,* which means "school") is a method for applying the tools of "dialectic" or rational analysis to the elucidation of the revealed contents of faith. This type of theology emerged in conjunction with the development of universities during the High Middle Ages, and the beginning of theology as an academic discipline (*scientia*) in the university is to be sought here. Its two greatest representatives were Anselm of Canterbury (ca. 1033–1109) and Thomas Aquinas (ca. 1225–1274). Comparison of these two figures is instructive since Anselm stood in the Platonic tradition of Augustine, while Thomas made the daring move to appropriate the newly rediscovered philosophy of Aristotle (384–322 B.C.E.), which had been introduced into Western Europe through Muslim Spain. One question posed by both Anselm and Thomas is the extent to which reason can know the truths of faith apart from revelation. Because of their differing philosophical views, Anselm and Thomas gave contrasting answers to this question.

Unlike the Greek theologians, Augustine did not use the word *theology* because of its pagan connotations as that branch of philosophy that deals with the gods. But he obviously affirmed the necessity of employing reason in the service of the truth of the Catholic faith. As he grew more suspicious of the mind's capacity to know truth unless it is aided by divine revelation, he increasingly emphasized the necessity of faith—understood as intellectual assent to the doctrines of the church—as the beginning of inquiry. He quoted Isa. 7:9 in the old Latin version that read: "Unless you believe, you will not understand." Anselm popularized this understanding of theology as "faith seeking understanding" (*fides quaerens intellectum*), and this has become the most influential view of theology's task in both Catholicism and Protestantism. He wrote: "I do not seek to understand in order to believe, but I believe in order to understand" (*credo ut intelligam*).[13] In applying the tools of reason, the scholastics were not in any way deviating from this understanding of theology. Reason, for them, was not the source of doctrine; it only provided the tools by which to understand doctrine, which was believed to be divinely revealed in the scriptures and authoritatively taught by the church's magisterium in Rome. But, through the application of these dialectical tools, they hoped to resolve some knotty puzzles bequeathed to them by the tradition.

There was, apparently, no theological problem too daunting for Anselm's brilliant mind. He asked: how can God be almighty and yet unable to do certain things? For instance, it is impossible for God to tell a lie. Anselm answered: the so-called power to lie is really evidence of powerlessness on the part of the liar. But God can do nothing through a lack of power. Therefore, God's inability to tell a lie only serves to confirm that God is truly almighty. Another question posed by Anselm is this: how can God be both compassionate and eternally unchangeable or impassible? The terms stand in apparent contradiction to one another, since compassion requires the ability to feel or be moved by another's pain. Anselm resolved this problem by saying that God is compassionate according to our perception but not according to God's being. We say that God is compassionate because he saves sinners, even though God does not feel any emotions. Another conundrum: how can God be merciful if he is truly just? Is it not unjust to spare the wicked? Anselm's answer: God's goodness is incomprehensible and includes both his justice and his mercy. Goodness is a larger category than justice to describe God, so we have to understand the attributes of justice and mercy as dual expressions of the divine goodness.[14] Anselm also wanted to understand how there can be many attributes of God (for example, life, wisdom, truth, goodness, blessedness, and eternity) if God is not composite. These attributes cannot refer to different parts of God since God is absolutely one and, hence, not made up of parts. Therefore, the many attributes are different names for the whole of God: "Thus life and wisdom and the rest are not parts of thee, but all are one, and each of them is the whole that thou art, and what all the rest are."[15] Similarly, Anselm explained that, though God exists neither in time nor in place, God contains all times and all places.[16]

Anselm even asked: why did God, who is almighty, take upon himself the weakness of human nature in the incarnation? Could not God have saved humankind in some other way? The answer: No, it was necessary for God to become human on account of the dilemma created by the fall. Since sin was an offense of infinite proportion to the divine honor, reparation (atonement) for this debt needed to be infinite; and, although it was right and just that human beings should pay back this infinite debt to God, only God—being infinite— was capable of doing it. Hence, it was necessary that God become human to order to satisfy the requirement of divine justice on behalf of those who owed it but were incapable of meeting it. Anselm's confidence in the rationality of the Catholic faith is nowhere better expressed than here, since he believed he had adduced "necessary reasons" to demonstrate—even to those who had never heard of Christ—that salvation could have come by no other route.[17]

Anselm's greatest legacy, however, is the "onto-logical argument" for the existence of God. It is a strictly rational demonstration since it proceeds by means of logical deduction from the very concept of God and does not depend upon any knowledge mediated by experience. Anselm begins his quest to understand the intrinsic rationality of faith in God with a prayer that fully illustrates the Augus-tinian view of theology as "faith seeking understanding": "O Lord, since thou givest understanding to faith, give me to understand . . . that thou dost exist, as we believe. . . ." He then defines God as "a being than which none greater can be thought." The point of this definition is to exclude the possibility of God's nonexistence. He cites scripture: "The fool hath said in his heart, 'There is no God'" (Ps. 14:1). Once the fool hears this definition, however, he cannot possibly deny that God exists. Why? Because "that than which a greater cannot be thought" must exist not only in the mind (*in intellectu*) but also in reality (*in re*). If God exists only in the mind, a greater being than God can be thought, namely, a being that exists not merely in the mind but in reality as well. Since, however, God is, by definition, perfect, and since perfection includes existence, God must possess "existence" as an attribute.

This argument has been rejected by many philosophers (for example, Immanuel Kant) as logically fallacious. The fallacy lies in treating existence as a predicate, as though it added something to the definition of God. But other philosophers (for example, Charles Hartshorne) have pointed out that, while this formulation of the ontological argument is flawed, there is, in fact, a second formulation of the argument given by Anselm that is not vulnerable to this criticism. The second argument goes like this: God cannot be coherently conceived except as the one being whose existence is strictly necessary: "God cannot be thought of as not existing." To ask whether God exists, therefore, shows that one has not correctly grasped the concept of God. It would be similar to asking about a four-sided triangle! Hence, once the correct definition is granted, it is a contradiction in terms to ask if God exists. If, however, the fool continues to persist in his denial, then he shows himself to be not only a fool but, indeed, "a stupid fool" at that.[18]

Anselm's ontological argument reflects his philosophical roots in the Platonic tradition. But Thomas, being an Aristotelian, rejected the argument. The crucial difference between Anselm and Thomas on the question of the natural knowledge of God arises from their differing epistemologies or theories of knowledge. Anselm is a rationalist who believes in the possibility of *a priori* knowledge (that is, prior to experience) while Thomas is an empiricist who affirms only *a posteriori* knowledge (that is, from experience).

The Synthesis of Thomas

Thomas agreed with Anselm that God necessarily exists: God's essence is to exist, whereas existence does not belong to the essence of other existing things. But, for Thomas, reason unaided by revelation does not know this. Such knowledge has to be divinely revealed. This is how Thomas interpreted Exod. 3:14, where God reveals his name to Moses, saying, "I am that I am." Anselm is correct to affirm that God is, by definition, "He who is," but we only know this by virtue of revelation. Thomas distinguished between two forms of self-evidence: a proposition "may be self-evident in itself, but not self-evident to us."[19] The statement "God exists" is self-evident in itself because the subject and the predicate are identical; but this is not self-evident to reason.

This objection to Anselm reflects the distinction Thomas made between the order of being and the order of knowing. According to Thomas, causes precede their effects in the order of being. But, in the order of knowing, effects are known first and from there we move to knowledge of their causes. For example, the sphericity of the moon causes it to appear in phases, but the phases of the moon are what allow or cause us to conclude that it is a sphere. "We can demonstrate God's existence in this way, from his effects which are known to us, even though we do not know his essence."[20] On the basis of natural reason, we can know *that* God exists but not *what* God is. Since God can only be known from his effects, knowledge of God's existence—apart from revelation—can only proceed inductively, moving from the effects back to their cause. Thomas outlined five empirical—as distinct from solely rational—arguments or "ways" (*quinque viae*) to demonstrate God's existence. The five ways share a common logical structure. Each begins with observation of some feature of the world ("effect") and from there proceeds to infer God's existence ("cause"). Thomas concludes each argument by saying, "and this everyone understands to be God." In other words, his arguments are meant to clarify how we understand and employ the concept of God. The five ways are (1) the argument from motion: since all things are moved from a potential state to an actual state by other things, there must be a perfectly actual "first mover" unmoved by any other; (2) the argument from causality: since all things are effects of other causes, there must be a first efficient cause uncaused by anything else; (3) the argument from contingency: since all things exist contingently, there must be a necessary being who is the cause of their existence; (4) the argument from degrees: since all judgments of better and worse presuppose some standard of comparison, there must be an absolute standard of goodness, truth, beauty, etc.; and (5) the argument from design: since natural things lacking intelligence strive to realize ends or purposes, there must be some intelligent mind that directs them to their appropriate ends.[21]

According to Thomas, it is necessary that there should be a discipline founded upon revelation (theology or, as he called it, "sacred doctrine") just as there is one founded upon natural reason (philosophy). The former teaches the supernatural truths of the Catholic faith that have to be believed in order for persons to be saved. These truths exceed human reason. But reason is not destroyed by revelation. Revelation perfects reason, supplying what it cannot know about God (for example, God is a Trinity). And since not everyone is philosophically gifted, even those truths about God that can be known by the natural light of reason are also revealed (for example, God exists). So everything necessary for salvation is revealed by God, though some of the revealed truths can also be known by reason apart from revelation.[22] Unlike Anselm, Thomas didn't believe that the truths of Catholic faith can be given a demonstrative proof. But objections to the faith can be refuted because reason cannot conflict with revelation. Philosophy thus provides assistance to theology since reason stands in the service of revelation. The fundamental axiom of Thomism is "grace does not destroy nature, but perfects it." The relation of revelation to reason is illustrative of this axiom in the realm of epistemology: "Since therefore grace does not supplant nature, but perfects it, reason ought to be the servant of faith in the same way as the natural inclination of the will is the servant of charity."[23]

The idea that grace perfects nature presupposes a concept of "supernature." Human beings have both a natural and a supernatural end (that is, purpose or goal). The "cardinal" moral virtues taught by the philosophers pertain to our natural end: justice, temperance, courage, and wisdom. The "theological" virtues point us to our supernatural end since they have God as their object: faith, hope, and love. Given this distinction, Thomas can affirm that human beings in their natural state are capable of good works. But these deeds exemplifying the cardinal virtues are not meritorious for salvation. For that, we must bring forth the theological virtues; but apart from grace, this is not possible. In this way, grace perfects nature by adding something to it that is otherwise beyond itself.

The decision to appropriate Aristotle's philosophy was a bold move. Plato had always been the favorite philosopher of Christian theologians. The influence of Aristotle's metaphysical categories can be seen in the way Thomas speaks of God as "pure act, without any potentiality."[24] But Thomas was not simply influenced by Aristotle; he actually transformed Aristotle's philosophy in the process of appropriating it for Christian purposes. Even the neo-Platonic themes of Augustine are not absent in Thomas. So, for example, he clarified that whereas God's essence is to exist, creatures exist by virtue of their participation in being, which is a neo-Platonic emphasis. Yet in availing himself of Aristotelian categories to reinterpret this neo-Platonic Augustinian heritage, he was doing something potentially heretical since some of Aristotle's views stood in contradiction to the Catholic faith. Aristotle taught the eternity of the world, a doctrine that conflicts with the Christian view that the world was created and had a beginning. The way Thomas resolved this tension is indicative of his understanding of the relation between reason and revelation. The idea that the world has always existed is not impossible, Thomas admitted. But its truth has never been demonstrated, either. The idea that the world had a beginning is an article of faith, not a matter of science (as science was then understood). Yet if it could be proven that the world has always existed, Thomas did not think that even this would necessarily conflict with the doctrine of creation. If the world exists everlastingly, it does so only because of God's will that it always exist. The crucial distinction is between the world's everlasting duration and its absolute dependence upon God's will as the sole sufficient cause of everything that is.[25]

Thomas attended carefully to the problem of theological language. The medievals acknowledged a fourfold sense of scripture, which Thomas divided into two: the literal or historical sense and three kinds of spiritual sense (allegorical, tropological or moral, and anagogical or eschatological). Thomas insisted upon the priority of the literal sense and argued that the other three senses are founded upon it. Nonetheless, he explained that sometimes the literal sense of scripture is metaphorical as, for example, when scripture speaks of the arm of the Lord. The literal sense is not that God has a bodily member but that he has what such a figure of speech signifies, namely, active power.[26]

Thomas's most important contribution to a theory of language is his doctrine of analogy as the proper way to speak about God. Negative terms do not signify the being of God; rather, they express the distance of the creature from God. But positive terms really do signify God's being, even though they do it inadequately. Thomas distinguished between the perfections signified by analogies and their mode of signification:

> As regards what is signified by these names, they belong properly to God, and more properly than they belong to creatures, and are applied primarily to him. But as regards their mode of signification, they do not properly and strictly apply to God; for their mode of signification applies to creatures.[27]

Analogical language is neither univocal nor equivocal. On the one hand, analogical terms for God do not mean exactly the same thing as they do when applied to creatures. Thomas rejected the view—later to be defended by Duns Scotus—that a term such as *being* can be univocally predicated of both God and creatures. On the other hand, the attributes do not lose all continuity of meaning. So, for example, we say "God is wise," but we don't mean that God has learned a lot from his experiences over the centuries! Yet wisdom is truly predicated of God in a preeminent sense. The difference between metaphor and analogy is this: whereas the former is applied primarily to creatures and used to indicate a similar quality in God (for example, *arm* to indicate strength), the latter is applied primarily to God and only secondarily to creatures (for example, being, goodness, wisdom). Hence, analogical language is a *via eminentiae* that allows us to say something affirmatively about God while recognizing the difference of proportion in the meaning of a term when it is applied to God and creatures.

The contrast between Anselm and Thomas on the question of reason and revelation illustrates the point that any theologian who affirms the possibility of natural theology has to make a philosophical decision between competing epistemological approaches to the natural knowledge of God: either rationalism or empiricism. Then the relation between the natural knowledge of God and the revealed truths of faith has to be clarified, that is, whether the relation is one of identity or overlap. Furthermore, the relation between scholastic or academic theology and mystical or spiritual theology has to be addressed. Near the end of his life, Thomas had a mystical experience. From this vantage point, he looked back upon his attempt to understand the mysteries of faith with the tools of reason and dismissed it as nothing more than straw. Although controversial in his own time, Thomas would eventually win recognition as Roman Catholicism's greatest theologian and be known to posterity as the "angelic doctor."

6

The Protestant Reformation

The premise of medieval theology and spirituality is that we have to become holy before we can be accepted by God, who is holy. Only after we have been perfectly sanctified (i.e, made holy) in faith, hope, and love, shall we be justified in God's sight. Of course, we cannot bring forth these meritorious works apart from the infusion of grace through the sacraments. Grace is here understood as "sanctifying grace," which makes the sinner pleasing to God (*gratia gratum faciens*). But the late medieval period witnessed an important shift in religious sensibility that was characterized by a deep anxiety about sin and the fear of damnation. This led to a quest for certainty about salvation that was not to be had through the church's sacramental mediation of grace.

Julian and the Goodness of God

Julian of Norwich (1342–ca. 1423) is an exemplary figure for indicating the nature of this shift. Julian was a mystic who sought a direct experience of God. Like many women in the medieval period,

Julian expressed her theological insights by writing a text recounting and interpreting her mystical visions since the other genres of theological literature were written by men in positions of ecclesial and academic leadership from which women were excluded. Julian anticipated that her claim to have received direct revelations or "showings of divine love" would be met with suspicion on account of the medieval devaluation of women. Hence, she tried to assure her readers that she presumes neither to teach ("for I am a woman, ignorant, weak and frail") nor in any way to challenge "the true doctrine of Holy Church." Nonetheless, she asked: "But because I am a woman, ought I therefore to believe that I should not tell you of the goodness of God, when I saw at that same time that it is his will that it be known?"[1]

On the basis of her mystical experience, Julian proclaimed that salvation is certain and not to be doubted. "All will be well" because God is "very accessible, familiar and courteous" and "wants to be trusted."[2] The sinner need not fear divine wrath since God cannot be angry. Wrath is a human trait that stems from a lack of power, wisdom, and goodness. This lack is on our part, not God's. God does not even blame us for our sin. Indeed, sin is not a moral failing at all but a constriction of our perspective, which prevents us from seeing clearly just how much God loves us. She illustrated this theology with a parable about a servant hastening to do his master's business. While underway, the servant falls into a ditch. Stuck in the ditch, he cannot accurately perceive the disposition of his master toward him. He incorrectly assumes that his master is angry with him when, in fact, the master is graciously disposed toward him. The fall into the ditch was not evidence of pride but was simply an accident occasioned by the servant's zeal to serve his master. The greatest affliction in all this was the servant's lack of consolation resulting from his inaccurate perception of his master's attitude toward him.[3]

Corresponding to this view of sin as a constriction in our perspective, Julian suggested that salvation is also a matter of perspective. Sin is a form of blindness, whereas salvation is a recovery of sight. In our blindness we incorrectly assume that God is angry with us. With renewed sight we correctly perceive God's character as loving and gracious. Herein lay Julian's assurance of salvation. Unlike the church's doctrine, which taught that grace makes sinners pleasing to God by transforming them into saints, Julian's perspectival approach reversed this completely so that, now, grace makes God pleasing to the sinner. Salvation does not consist in a process of sanctification whereby we must first become holy in order to be acceptable to God on Judgment Day; rather, it consists in a shift in our perspective from viewing God as angry to viewing God as loving.

Julian also wished to contemplate "motherhood in God" and employed this image to make her fundamental point about sin and salvation:

> This fair lovely word "mother" is so sweet and so
> kind in itself that it cannot truly be said of anyone
> or to anyone except of him and to him who is the
> true Mother of life and of all things. To the prop-
> erty of motherhood belong nature, love, wisdom
> and knowledge, and this is God.[4]

Sometimes the mother must allow the child to fall
and to feel distress, but this is for its own benefit;
she can never tolerate any real harm to come to her
child. So sin is necessary, "for if we did not fall, we
should not know how feeble and how wretched we
are in ourselves, nor, too, should we know so completely the wonderful love of our Creator."[5] Julian
also spoke of Jesus as "our mother" because he
gives us the new spiritual birth.

Although Julian did not wish to teach anything
heretical, her theology did, in fact, deviate from the
church's doctrine since it offered an immediate
assurance of salvation apart from the sacramental
mediation of grace. But there was another problem
as well: Julian failed to see any distinction between
God and our substance in her vision. Julian is
aware of the problem and does not want to be
heretical on this score: "And I saw no difference
between God and our substance, but, as it were, all
God; and still my understanding accepted that our
substance is in God, that is to say that God is God,
and our substance is a creature in God."[6] Mysticism
has always posed a problem for the monotheistic
traditions, since the mystical union can lead to
abolition of the difference between creator and the
creature.

Martin Luther's Gracious God

Martin Luther (1483–1546) was wrestling with the same issue of certainty when he asked, "How can I find a gracious God?" The Reformation was born out of the new interpretation of the Bible to which Luther came after searching for an answer to his own quest for assurance of salvation. According to Luther, the main doctrine of scripture is justification by faith alone (*sola fide*). This was a break with the Catholic doctrinal tradition, even though Luther claimed to have Augustine on his side. What distinguished Protestants from other reform-minded persons in the late medieval era was the conviction that all abuses in the church stemmed from a faulty doctrine taught by the church's tradition. Hence, the church's doctrine must be *re*-formed by returning to scripture alone (*sola scriptura*). In their exposition of the Bible, the Protestants rejected allegorical exegesis entirely in favor of the grammatical or literal sense of the text. They also insisted upon reading the Bible in the original languages of Hebrew and Greek, setting aside the Latin *Vulgate* as a flawed translation.

Luther was a friar who had been trained in the scholastic tradition of theology. But this was not the scholasticism of Thomas Aquinas, which Luther appears not to have known. It was, rather, the *via moderna* of the fourteenth and fifteenth centuries, called either nominalism or Occamism after William of Occam (ca. 1280–ca. 1349). The nominalists taught that God made a covenant with humanity according to which "God does not deny grace to those who do what is in them" (*facientibus quod in se est*). This means that, in a state of sin, a person can do both good works (which Thomas affirmed) and "congruous" merits (which Thomas denied). A congruous merit is not a full merit, though it is "fitting" for God to treat it as meritorious; since God sees that we are doing all we can to be righteous, God rewards us with grace. On the basis of grace, we are then enabled to earn our salvation on the basis of "condign" merits, that is, merits in the full sense of the word. Predestination, in this theology, means God's foreknowledge of who will do all they can to "merit," so to speak, the first infusion of grace. Luther condemned this theology as Pelagian. Grace and merit are antithetical concepts, he argued, and cannot be harmonized. Thomas had wielded these terms in a completely different manner. He said that, in a state of grace, we perform acts that can be considered either as condign or congruous merits, depending upon the perspective from which they are viewed: insofar as God's grace effects these works, they are condign merits since whatever God does is worthy of full merit; but insofar as they reflect our cooperation with grace, these same works can only be said to merit grace congruously.[7] Thomas would surely have agreed with Luther that the nominalist doctrine was Pelagian. If Luther had known of Thomas, he could not have condemned all of scholastic theology as a betrayal of Augustine's insistence upon *sola gratia*.

For Luther, the issue was not about an overly subtle distinction to be debated by academics. It was, first and foremost, an existential matter of highest urgency. He charged that any theology encouraging sinners to confide in their own powers and merits leads to despair since we can never know for certain that we have, in fact, done all that is within us. Indeed, this had been Luther's personal experience with a bad conscience as a result of his attempt to live the monastic life. Insofar as salvation depended in any way upon his own efforts, he could never rid himself of the gnawing doubt that there remained some sin he had forgotten to confess. Even though the nominalist theology was intended to provide some pastoral guidance for souls seeking to navigate the earthly pilgrimage by telling them what *they* could do to avoid hell, Luther needed an assurance that his salvation lay completely in God's hands and not even partially in his own!

On the way to his new insight into the meaning of justification, Luther struggled to understand what Paul meant by writing, "The righteousness of God is revealed in the gospel" (Rom. 1:17). Luther couldn't understand this. Hadn't God's righteousness already been revealed under the law? Furthermore, why is this "good news"? It is bad news for the sinner who has to stand before the heavenly judge with a guilty conscience. Even more perplexing was Paul's citation of Habakkuk 2:4, "The righteous shall live by faith." Why do the righteous live by faith when they have their own righteousness on which to depend? Luther solved his own puzzle by proposing that "God's righteousness" does not mean the "active righteousness" taught in

the law by which God as a just judge condemns
and punishes sinners. No, when the gospel declares
God's righteousness to have been revealed
"through faith for faith," it refers to the "passive
righteousness" God gives to sinners as a gift on
account of Christ's merits.[8] That's why the righteous are said to live by faith, precisely because
they do not have their own righteousness of which
to boast. The righteous live by faith in the trustworthiness of God's promise to forgive sinners for
Christ's sake and to reckon their faith as righteousness. For this reason, justification is by faith alone
apart from works of the law.

Luther's crucial distinction between law and
gospel provided him with the key with which to
interpret scripture. The gospel stands in an antithetical relationship to the law. The law teaches that we
should merit our salvation by good works (Luther
does not distinguish between good works and merits, as did Thomas). The gospel teaches that salvation is through faith, not works. The law shows us
God as a judge who condemns us in our sin. This is
the "alien" work of God. The gospel brings forth
God as a father who graciously forgives our sin.
This is the "proper" work of God. Luther concluded
that the law was given, not that we might save ourselves by works, but that we might see how sinful
we are through our inability to fulfill its demands.
Only after we have come to despair of ourselves are
we ready to rely completely upon the mercy of God
revealed in the gospel. Thus, God does his alien
work in the law for the sake of his proper work in

the gospel. The distinction between law and gospel is not identical to that between the Old and the New Testaments, since gospel is found in the Old Testament just as law is taught in the New Testament. While this theology resembles that of Marcion in its contrast between the ways of salvation signified by law and gospel, Luther did not pit the New Testament against the Old as did the second-century heretic.

Still, Luther was heretical in his own right, for his theology deviated in crucial respects from that taught by the Roman church. The doctrine of "faith alone" is a denial of the Catholic doctrine that we are justified by "faith formed by love" (*fides caritate formata*), according to which "unformed faith," that is, faith not perfected by works of love, is insufficient for justification (1 Cor. 13:2). By contrast, Luther taught "faith active in love" (Gal. 5:6). Faith is inherently active and expresses itself outwardly in works of love toward the neighbor. Whereas the "inner person" stands before God in a relation of faith alone apart from works, the "outer person" stands before the neighbor in a relation of love, where works are necessary to meet the needs of the neighbor. The paradox of Christian existence is that we are freed from works in relation to God yet obligated to works of love in relation to the neighbor. But these works of love do not give us something of which to boast before God on Judgment Day. They are merely the outward expression of gratitude for God's free mercy through Christ.[9] With this distinction, Luther argued that the basic problem in Catholic theology was its confusion of justification with the goal of the process of sanctification. In Luther's theology, by contrast, sanctification is not a prerequisite to our justification: we are simultaneously sinners and yet righteous on account of faith (*simul iustus et peccator*).

Like Julian, Luther asked for an assurance of salvation. He, too, broke with the medieval assumption that we must first become holy in order to stand before a holy God. They both understood grace as God's mercy, not as a supernatural substance that makes the sinner pleasing to God. For Luther, the sacraments do not convey a sanctifying grace *ex opere operato*; instead, they serve as pledges to confirm the trustworthiness of God's promise of forgiveness to sinners.[10] Faith is trust in this promise, in contrast to the Catholic view, which treated faith as intellectual assent to the church's doctrine. Since faith comes from hearing the gospel (Rom. 10:17), the sermon is central to Protestant worship. Like Julian, Luther thus developed a perspectival approach to the knowledge of God's graciousness. And for both of them, the assurance that God is gracious was sufficient to put an end to the anxiety about damnation that haunted their age.

Luther's language about God is paradoxical. God is both hidden and revealed. Hiddenness has two distinct meanings: first, God transcends his revelation to us, so we cannot know everything about God; second, God remains transcendent even in his revelation to us. According to the first sense, finite creatures cannot encounter the naked power of God, which would overwhelm us. According to the second sense, God reveals himself to us in ambiguous ways, hiding his glory under signs of humility (for example, in the manger at Bethlehem or on the cross at Golgotha). He thereby makes room for faith since God gives himself to us in a manner that goes against the expectations of reason. The object of theology for Luther is not God *a se*, or in himself, but only as he reveals himself to us in the gospel (*pro nobis* or for us). We must not try to look at God behind his revelation; we must instead cling to Christ as the revelation of God, for therein do we find our only assurance that God is merciful. Apart from his revelation, God is utterly mysterious in the manner in which he rules nature and history (Isa. 45:15). There is a parallel here to the nominalists' distinction between God's absolute power (*potentia absoluta*) and his ordained power (*potentia ordinata*), between what God can do and what he has chosen to do. They insisted that God was under no necessity to bring about salvation in any particular way, so it is not possible for human reason to comprehend God within its own categories (contra Anselm). For Luther, assurance of salvation is found solely in the revelation of God's predestinating grace, which is paradoxically hidden under the cross of Christ. But why does God, who shows his mercy in Christ, harden the hearts of so many? Here Luther is up against the mystery of God hidden behind his revelation.[11]

John Calvin and God's Glory

John Calvin (1509–1564), a second-generation reformer, developed Luther's theology and gave it a systematic form. In virtually all major points, Calvin followed Luther's lead. But there were a few differences. Unlike Luther, Calvin believed that, while one purpose of the law is to drive sinners to despair, God's primary purpose in giving us the law is to instruct believers in the duties of the Christian life.[12] Calvin thus placed more weight on the notion of sanctification than did Luther, but this does not mean that he denied Luther's fundamental point about justification. There is also Calvin's departure from Luther as to how Christ is present in the Lord's Supper. Calvin denied what Luther affirmed, namely, Christ's resurrected body shares in the attribute of omnipresence by virtue of the *communicatio idiomatum* or "exchange of attributes" between the divine and human natures. Calvin called this ancient principle of predication a "figure of speech."[13] For Calvin, the Holy Spirit makes possible our communion with the body and blood of Jesus, which are in heaven. Otherwise, Calvin is a Lutheran.

Unlike Luther, Calvin had not been a monk. Instead, Calvin came to his theological studies with the background of a humanist scholar deeply steeped in the Greek and Latin classics. Calvin's first book was a commentary upon the Stoic philosopher, Seneca (ca. 4 B.C.E.–65 C.E.). Calvin's distinctive contribution to the Reformation lay in his combination of Lutheran theology with Renaissance humanism. The paradox of the "Reformed" tradition of Calvin is that, while there has been more of a tendency toward biblicism than one finds in Lutheranism, there has also been greater openness to philosophy and secular learning.

For Calvin, the ideal for human existence is "piety" (*pietas*), reverence for and love of God which the knowledge of his benefits calls forth.[14] *Piety* was the term employed by the ancients to describe proper religion as distinct from both superstition and atheism. Everything God created is a mirror in which the divine glory is reflected. The human being is unique in that it was created for self-conscious praise of its creator.[15] Calvin affirmed that God has planted "a seed of religion" or "a sense of divinity" in all persons, so that no one has any excuse for not honoring God as God. After Adam's fall, the seed of religion is thwarted in its growth by superstition and the sense of divinity is transferred to objects other than God. Hence, no one is truly an atheist since everyone worships something, as is evident from the fact that no society, however barbaric, has ever been bereft of some religion or other.[16] Faith in the gospel is the way piety is restored after the fall so that God may be given the honor he is due. The sense of God's glory and majesty pervades Calvin's theology. He emphatically rejected the idea that a pious person is motivated to serve God in order to be saved. Salvation is a by-product of a proper fear of God. We do not live for ourselves. We belong to God. [17] Whereas Luther's driving concern was to find a gracious God, Calvin's central interest lay in discerning how the human being can be placed in the service of God.

Calvin's mature theology is structured by two principles. The first is the close interrelation between knowledge of God and self. One cannot truly know the one without knowing the other.[18] The second is a "twofold knowledge of God" as creator and redeemer. To this there corresponds a twofold form of self-knowledge as created and redeemed.[19] No more than Luther did Calvin think we could know God in his aseity. We can only know God as he accommodates himself to us. The created order of nature is God's accommodation to us as finite, whereas God's word in scripture is God's accommodation to us as sinful. If Adam hadn't fallen, we would have known God's goodness through his creation. But since our eyes have been blinded from perceiving the benevolence of God, we have to hear God address us through his word, where he condescends to our level by speaking to us as parents speak to infants. Scripture is like a pair of spectacles with which we can see clearly again.[20] Thereby God shows himself once again as our creator and now also as our redeemer in Christ. The person of piety (or faith) trusts that God is a generous "father" who looks after his children's welfare and looks to God as "the fountain of all good things" (*fons omnium bonorum*).[21]

Providence is a theme of special importance in Calvin's theology since it is bound up with the knowledge of God as creator: "unless we pass over to his providence . . . we do not yet properly grasp what it means to say: 'God is creator.'"[22] This is because, unlike profane persons, the pious see God's power evident in the continuing course of events and not merely at their inception. Yet not only does God preserve all things in being, but he also nourishes and cares for everything he has made, including the least sparrow (Matt. 10:29).[23] Ignorance of providence is the ultimate of miseries, since the events of nature and history do not make sense to us apart from this knowledge. Calvin does not mean God's foreknowledge since "providence is lodged in the act." Indeed, God "so regulates all things that nothing takes place without his deliberation."[24] With faith in God's sovereign governance of all events, the pious person can be certain that, just "when the world appears to be aimlessly tumbled about, the Lord is everywhere at work." Indeed, "nothing can befall except he determine it."[25] What appears fortuitous to our minds is ordained by God's decree; nothing happens by chance. When we observe that "some mothers have full and abundant breasts, but others' are almost dry," we must conclude that "God wills to feed one [infant] more liberally, but another more meagerly."[26] Yet everything God does is just, even though we may not understand how this is so. Indeed, the elect are assured that all things are ultimately for their benefit. In the midst of adversity, the pious heart takes comfort in knowing that God "will not suffer anything to happen but what may turn out to its good and salvation."[27]

Calvin easily distinguished his view of God's ceaseless activity from that of the ancient Epicureans, for whom the gods were idle and did nothing. It was more difficult for him to clarify the difference between his view of providence and the Stoic doctrine of fate. Given his deterministic view of the divine omni-causality, it is not a simple matter, and he noted that the same problem beset Augustine. On the one hand, Calvin explained that he wasn't interested in quibbling over a single word. On the other hand, he clarified that "we do not, with the Stoics, contrive a necessity out of the perpetual connection and intimately related series of causes, which is contained in nature."[28] Calvin's meaning appears to be that the universe is not ultimately governed by an impersonal causality. Nonetheless, he came close to the Stoic equation of God with nature when he wrote: "I confess, of course, that it can be said piously, provided that it proceeds from a pious mind, that nature is God (*naturam esse deum*)." Calvin hastened to add, however, that it is "a harsh and improper saying," since it confuses God with "the inferior course of his works."[29] He was concerned lest profane persons use "nature" in place of "God" as a pretext for their lack of gratitude to the "fountain of all good things." Furthermore, Calvin did acknowledge the reality of secondary causes, and he explained that God sometimes works through them, sometimes without them, and sometimes even contrary to them. Still, however much Calvin wanted to distinguish God from nature, he emphasized God's intimate involvement with every detail of nature's operation. Nothing, for Calvin, could be attributed to a natural cause without its also being attributed to divine causality.

The Reformation principle of "scripture alone" was not without its ambiguities. The Protestants placed all their authority in scripture since it is divinely inspired, whereas "popes and councils can err." The Catholics retorted that the canon of scripture was determined by the orthodox tradition in its fight against heresy. If the inspiration of tradition is denied, the authority of scripture falls to the ground. This was a difficult argument to refute, and the best the Protestants could come up with was simply to affirm that the Word of God had called the church into being, not the other way around! There was also the problem that the Protestants could not agree among themselves as to what scripture teaches, in spite of their insistence upon its clarity or "perspicuity." The debates between the Lutherans and the Reformed on matters of sacramental theology showed just how problematic the Protestant principle of biblical authority truly was. Who's to decide, the Catholics wanted to know, *which* interpretation of the Bible is the correct one? But nowhere was the relation between scripture and tradition more problematic than in the question of trinitarianism. Michael Servetus (1511–1553), a forerunner of modern Unitarianism, denied the doctrine of the Trinity, which he insisted was not scriptural. Servetus had hoped to convince Calvin of this position, but, instead, was burned at the stake in Geneva. Yet, oddly enough, Calvin himself had been accused of "Arianism" by a fellow Protestant, Pierre Caroli (1481–1545). While the charge was baseless, Calvin's refusal to give in to Caroli's demand that he subscribe to the ancient creeds only reinforced the suspicion of a lack of orthodoxy on his part. No doubt, Calvin did not want to attribute to the church's postbiblical tradition an authority that would violate his principle of "scripture alone." But there is more to it than that.[30]

The tension for Calvin arose out of his preference for scriptural language, on the one hand, and his rejection of "speculation" in favor of a "theology within the limits of piety alone," on the other.[31] Calvin conceded that nonscriptural terms such as *homoousion* are useful insofar as they function to sniff out heretics, and he did think nonbiblical terminology could be helpful to clarify those passages in the Bible that are difficult to understand.[32] Yet Calvin was nervous about wanting to know more about God than had been revealed in scripture. As an example of unwarranted speculation Calvin cited "that Dionysius, whoever he was" and judged his writings to be "for the most part nothing but talk."[33] Even the revered Augustine received Calvin's disapproval for his speculation that the human soul in its relations of understanding, will, and memory was a reflection of the Trinity.[34] The knowledge of God approved by Calvin is that which edifies us in the duties of piety. Hence, it is eminently practical, not theoretical.

> What is God? Men who pose this question are
> merely toying with idle speculation. It is more
> important for us to know of what sort he is and
> what is consistent with his nature. . . . Rather, our
> knowledge should serve first to teach us fear and
> reverence; secondly, with it as our guide and
> teacher, we should learn to seek every good from
> him, and, having received it, to credit it to his
> account.[35]

For this reason, Calvin set up this rule as his guide:
"Indeed, we shall not say that, properly speaking,
God is known where there is no religion or piety."[36]
Karl Barth correctly assessed Calvin's view of the
matter when he wrote: "it was only to the extent
that the doctrine of the Trinity could be understood
as practical knowledge that it seemed to him to be
scriptural and acceptable."[37]

In the early seventeenth century, Calvin's teaching received yet one more challenge. Jacob
Arminius (1560–1609), a Dutch Reformed pastor
who had studied in Geneva with Calvin's successor,
Theodore Beza (1519–1605), questioned the
Calvinist doctrine of predestination. Arminius
came to believe that God's grace is universally
offered to all and sinners have the freedom to
respond in faith to the gospel. Like nominalism,
Arminianism revived the semi-Pelagian position of
the earlier Augustine before he had decided that
even faith itself is a gift of God's predestinating
grace. And like Pelagius, Arminius objected that
Calvin's view made God the author of sin and
negated human freedom. After his death, the disci-

ples of Arminius presented his teachings to the public in a document called the *Remonstrance* and requested that a synod be convened to debate the issues. In 1618, the Synod of Dort condemned Arminianism and set forth what has since come to be known as orthodox Calvinism. This teaching was later made famous as "the five points of Calvinism," which can easily be remembered by the acronym TULIP. They are (1) total depravity, (2) unconditional election, (3) limited atonement (4) irresistible grace, and (5) perseverance of the saints. In other words, (1) after the fall, we do not have freedom to respond in faith, (2) God's election is not conditioned by any foreknowledge of our merits, (3) Christ's atoning death availed only for the elect, (4) grace cannot be rejected, and (5) the elect can never lose their salvation. The Arminian position can be understood as the converse of each of these five points. The most influential figure to popularize the Arminian viewpoint in the English-speaking world was John Wesley (1703–1791), the founder of Methodism.[38]

The period of the Reformation belongs to the larger story of medieval Christianity in the West. Up until the seventeenth century, the central issues remained the questions with which Augustine had wrestled, namely, how to understand grace and faith, divine election and human freedom, justification and sanctification. But the ambiguities he bequeathed to the West eventuated in the formation of two competing ways to construe his legacy. Moreover, the presuppositions of the Reformers were thoroughly medieval. Like the Catholics, the Protestants assumed that the Bible is divinely inspired and speaks with one voice through the medium of its human authors. Unlike the Catholics, however, the Protestants disputed the divine authorization of the postbiblical tradition of the church, though even they did not reject this tradition entirely. Still, their principle of "scripture alone" raised serious issues regarding religious authority since Protestantism gave rise to many interpretations of the Bible and thus failed to be a unified movement. Ironically, the Protestant quest for certainty of salvation issued in hermeneutical uncertainty regarding the interpretation of scripture. The problem of biblical authority became even more difficult as the insistence upon the literal sense of the biblical text led to the development of the historical-critical method in the modern era.

7

The Enlightenment and the Modern Era

The Enlightenment gave rise to a critique, on the basis of reason, of the inherited medieval religious traditions. The scientific revolution of the seventeenth and eighteenth centuries had occasioned a dramatic shift in the Western view of the cosmos. Nicholas Copernicus (1473–1543) and Galileo Galilei (1564–1642) challenged the traditional Ptolemaic conception of a geocentric universe. Galileo ran afoul of the Inquisition and was forced to recant in 1633. Yet the new (and eventually triumphant) heliocentric theory had important implications for Western religious sensibility and thought. On the one hand, it contradicted the cosmology presupposed by the Bible (Josh. 10:12-13). On the other hand, it rent asunder the harmony between cosmology and soteriology. If the earth isn't the center of the universe, then humanity is displaced from its central role in the cosmic drama. The heliocentric view thus generated a new religious question: instead of seeking certainty of salvation, persons sought to discern the meaning and purpose of humanity in such a vast cosmos.

The God of Reason

Isaac Newton (1642–1727) intensified this shift through his formulation of the law of gravity, which implied an understanding of nature as a law-governed nexus of cause and effect. No longer could events in the natural world (for example, bad harvests, earthquakes, or illness) be interpreted as signs of God's wrath, since nature has its own internal principles of explanation, which can be empirically observed and formulated with mathematical precision. Nevertheless, the scientific revolution did not exclude the idea of deity altogether but, rather, transformed it. Specifically, it raised the question of "miracles" and the mode of God's action in the world. Because the universe was now seen as like a machine that runs according to its own laws, God became viewed as the extra-mundane designer of the world-machine who set it in motion and left it free to run its own course.

Deism (from the Latin word for "God," *deus*) gave influential expression to the new religious sensibility and its corresponding view of deity. The deists advocated a purely rational and moral religion that they believed was also the original "natural religion" of humanity before it had become corrupted through superstitious error and clerical manipulation of the uneducated masses. Its tenets were summarized by Herbert of Cherbury (1583–1648) as follows: (1) the existence of one God, (2) God deserves our worship, (3) the practice of virtue is the chief part of the worship of God, (4) we must abhor evil and repent of our sins, and (5) there will be rewards for virtue and punishments for vice after death.[1] Not all deists rejected the idea of revelation entirely, but they did insist that the criterion of reason be applied to any purported claim on its behalf. One has to appreciate the earnestness of their rational religion in light of the fact that the Reformation had split Western Christendom into warring factions. Not only was there division between Catholic and Protestant, both of which claimed to represent the true Christian faith by appealing to their contradictory sources of authority; but also among the Protestants themselves there was no consensus as to how to interpret their own ultimate authority, the Bible. The hope that reason might overcome these religious differences was an idea whose time had come. Deism did, in fact, encourage religious tolerance and lent support to those who advocated for the separation of church and state.[2]

The only problem for a rational religion that purports to be based solely on an argument from natural theology is that it has to make good on its claims when tested against its own stated criteria: reason and experience. David Hume (1711–1776) gave the most sustained critical attention to the logic of the teleological argument for a designer of the world that constituted the heart of the deist position. This argument was the fifth of Thomas Aquinas's "five ways." The crux of Hume's objection to the teleological argument was that it wants to prove more than the evidence warrants. He pointed out the lack of proportionality between a finite effect and an infinite cause. Thomas had already recognized the force of the objection, but he did not make the argument from natural theology bear the religious weight it carried for the deists, since Thomas believed that reason unaided by supernatural revelation was insufficient to know God's essence.[3]

The logical structure of the teleological argument is based upon its use of analogy. If we see a beautiful house, we infer that it was designed by a talented architect. So, too, the deist looks at the world and infers that it must have a wise designer. Hence, the world is to a house as God is to an architect. But Hume argued that the analogy is not very exact since the world is only very remotely like a house. Besides, we have experience of only one world, whereas we have repeated experiences of houses. Moreover, the analogy is useless because it does not give us the sort of deity a religious person finds meaningful. If we take the analogy seriously, do we not have to suppose that God, like an architect, is finite and capable of error? Furthermore, why not assume the existence of many gods, just as there are many builders? And given the obvious imperfections of the world, should we not conclude that this world is perhaps the first attempt of some infantile deity or maybe even the product of senility on the part of some old deity? In any case, we could never prove from the evidence in the world that its designer was perfect in wisdom, goodness, and power. The most we can say is that the world has some cause or other, but this is not the deity required by religious belief.[4]

Hume also challenged the historical veracity of deism's claim that the earliest religion of humankind was a monotheism based upon the evidences of orderly design in the universe. Instead, he argued, polytheism was the earliest form of human religion. Also, religion arose out of elemental emotions of fear and hope in response to the unknown forces governing the world, not as a result of reasoned reflection upon cosmic order. Finally, Hume struck a blow to the deist notion that religion furthers morality by pointing to the many atrocities committed in the name of religion and even suggesting that ancient polytheism had been more tolerant than monotheism ever was.[5]

The deists weren't the only target of Hume's skepticism. He also called into question the basis for the orthodox belief in miracles which, for him, would mean an interruption of the observed orderliness of nature. But, while Hume himself did not believe in miracles, he did not categorically rule out the possibility of miracles altogether. So, the question is not, "Are miracles possible?" but, rather, "Under what conditions are we justified in believing a claim that a miracle has occurred?" According to Hume, we are justified in believing such a claim only so far as it is warranted by the evidence. Thus it becomes a matter of probability. If Peter claimed that he had seen the risen Jesus after his crucifixion, then the improbability of a dead man returning to life has to be weighed against the credibility of Peter as a witness. In other words, in order to credit his claim, it would have to be more improbable that

Peter could be wrong. As Hume put it, "No testimony is sufficient to establish a miracle unless the testimony be of such a kind that its falsehood would be more miraculous than the fact which it endeavors to establish."[6]

Immanuel Kant (1724–1804) said that reading Hume had awakened him from his "dogmatic slumbers" and led him to a critical assessment of the limits of reason. For Kant, a "transcendent" use of the mind's categories (for example, its notions of causality or substance) beyond their application to the data of sense experience is a mistake. There are definite limits to knowledge that reason may not transgress. Metaphysical ideas are thus not objects of knowledge. But Kant did not consider these ideas to be illusory, as did Hume. They serve an important heuristic purpose. The idea of God leads us to expand our knowledge of things to the fullest extent possible *as if* the world were a unity grounded in the creative purpose of an intelligent designer. The speculative ideas of pure reason are not "constitutive" of any object of our knowledge; rather, they function as "regulative" principles for systematizing our empirical knowledge.[7] Kant's significance is that he carried forward Hume's critique of natural theology and laid the foundation for a new approach to religious faith through his focus on the "turn to the subject."

What theoretical (or scientific) reason cannot know, practical (or moral) reason can postulate. Kant was also unlike Hume in sharing the deist conviction as to the importance of religious belief as a support for morality. For Kant, the moral life necessarily presupposes certain assumptions without which moral agency cannot be sustained. These postulates of practical reason are God, freedom, and immortality.[8] Clearly, the content of Kant's moral faith in God is the deist creed, but he defended it on other grounds. His faith is not a "rational religion" based on what reason can know of God; rather, it is a "reasonable religion" that keeps itself within the limits of reason.[9] Kant wrote, "I have therefore found it necessary to deny knowledge, in order to make room for faith."[10] He believed that Christianity came closest among the historical religions to embodying his ideal of a moral faith. Many Protestant theologians (for example, Albrecht Ritschl and Wilhelm Herrmann) followed Kant in rejecting natural theology and grounding faith in a consideration of the human subject's moral experience. Paul Tillich captured Kant's significance as "the philosopher of Protestantism" when he wrote: "There are three great philosophers and there are three great Christian groups: The Greek Orthodox whose philosopher's name is Plato; the Roman Catholics whose philosopher's name is Aristotle; and the Protestants whose philosopher's name is Kant."[11]

The Birth of Modern Theology

Friedrich Schleiermacher (1768–1834), considered to be the founder of modern theology, sought a different basis for religious faith entirely. He had been raised as a pietist and knew at first hand the dramatic experience of a heart "born again." But as he matured, Schleiermacher lost his youthful faith after his encounter with modern thought. Later, he found himself in the company of the Romantic circle, which cultivated the sense of "feeling" as the authentic mode of relating to the world, in reaction to the rationalism and moralism of the Enlightenment. The erstwhile pietist then made the daring move of reinterpreting religion as a form of feeling, specifically, the "sensibility and taste for the infinite."[12] "Feeling" here does not mean mere emotion but, rather, a prereflective awareness of the encompassing whole to which one belongs. Schleiermacher tried to argue with the Romantics on their own grounds. Against their rejection of religion in the name of culture (*Bildung*), he claimed they had failed to understand that religion is an essential aspect of human nature. Through this misunderstanding of religion, the Romantics misconstrued humanity itself, thereby leaving this dimension of life uncultivated. With this redefinition of religion as feeling, Schleiermacher believed himself to have reconciled the opposition between the religious heritage of his youth and the new worldview opened up by the Enlightenment.

Like Kant, Schleiermacher rejected metaphysics as the route to God. He argued that both traditional orthodoxy—which opposed the Enlightenment as antireligious—and the natural religion of deism—which looked upon the historic religious traditions as corrupted by superstition—operated with a faulty notion of religion as intellectual assent to theological propositions. The difference between them lay in the authoritative source of their respective theological beliefs: revelation versus reason. But, unlike Kant, Schleiermacher also rejected the moral route to faith in God based on the postulates of the practical reason and decried the aspiration for personal immortality as irreligious. For him, religion has its own autonomous sphere in feeling, which requires cultivation, just as do the spheres of science and morality; moreover, religion does not depend on the other spheres, nor does it exist to bolster them.

In speaking of religion as a sense and taste for the infinite, Schleiermacher was influenced by the revival of interest in Baruch Spinoza (1632–1677), the Jewish philosopher who had been excommunicated from the synagogue in Amsterdam on account of his heretical views. Spinoza's pioneering historical scholarship into the Bible led him to deny the Mosaic authorship of the Pentateuch.[13] To make matters worse, Spinoza refused to attribute personality to God and proposed, instead, a nonpersonal concept of deity. Many German thinkers who had already rejected the supernatural deity of orthodoxy remained dissatisfied with the extramundane artificer of the world propounded by the deists, and they found in Spinoza a way to conceive of God as *within* the world. In his criticism of deism, Hume had made an interesting, yet often overlooked, suggestion: instead of conceiving of God as an intelligent mind who relates externally to the world and imposes order on it from without, might it not be better to think of the world after the analogy of an organism that has its own principle of order within it? In this model, the deity is the soul of the world and the world is God's body.[14] Spinoza's pantheism articulated precisely such a view of God as the indwelling, not the transient, cause of the world. He distinguished between two senses of the word "nature": *natura naturans* ("nature naturing") is nature viewed as active, while *nature natured* is nature viewed as passive. God is to be understood in the first sense of nature as the active power by which all things come to be, whereas the world is nature in the second sense as all things that are thus brought forth.[15] Schleiermacher found in Spinoza a nonanthropomorphic alternative to both traditional theism and deism. Schleiermacher did not believe that the attribution of personality to God was essential to religion as he understood it. Hence, he could write of "the universe" or "the infinite" where one would ordinarily expect to read "God":

> The universe exists in uninterrupted activity and reveals itself to us every moment. Every form that it brings forth, every being to which it gives a separate existence according to the fullness of life, every occurrence that spills forth from its rich, ever-fruitful womb, is an action of the same upon us. Thus to accept everything individual as a part of the whole and everything limited as a representation of the infinite is religion.[16]

His Christian appropriation of Spinoza was brilliant, though controversial, since Spinozism was seen by many theologians as tantamount to atheism.[17]

In his mature statement of Protestant theology, Schleiermacher spoke of the essence of piety as "the consciousness of being absolutely dependent, or, which is the same thing, of being in relation with God."[18] God is "the Whence" *(das Woher)* of our feeling of absolute dependence. This consciousness of God becomes fully developed once an awareness is attained of living in a nature-system of entities with reciprocal relations of relative freedom and relative dependence. Schleiermacher maintained that God's absolute causality does not negate either the relative freedom or the relative dependence of finite agents: "It can never be necessary in the interest of religion so to interpret a fact that its dependence on God absolutely excludes its being conditioned by the system of nature."[19] To pit God's omnipotence against the interdependence of nature is a mistake, he argued. If the course of nature is divinely ordained, how can the divine power be said to be greater by altering what was originally decreed? Such an alteration could only be construed in a favorable light if the original design had been flawed, but this would imply some imperfection in God. Or there must be some power capable of offering resistance to God. But this, Schleiermacher claimed, would destroy our fundamental feeling of absolute dependence upon the divine causality. Hence, the most perfect representation of divine omnipotence

must reject a view of "miracle" as a divine interruption in the course of natural causality. A miracle is simply "the religious name for an event."[20]
Divine causality is, on the one hand, to be distinguished from the natural order and, on the other
hand, to be equated with it in scope.[21] For this reason, Schleiermacher believed that any conflict
between religion and science was based on a fundamental mistake, and he insisted on the need for
an "eternal covenant" between Christian faith and
modern science whereby each may pursue its
inquiries unhindered by interference from the
other.[22] He saw in the Reformation's disengagement
from the scholastic tradition a precedent for this
distinction between science and theology. Moreover, this line of argument explains how Schleiermacher understood the relation between pantheism
and monotheism. If pantheism means that no distinction between God and the world is drawn at
all, then it is inadequate. But, provided the distinction is made, the crucial point is that God and the
world belong together in our self-consciousness.
The ideal of piety consists in the ability to combine
every moment of consciousness of being in the
world with consciousness of the world's absolute
dependence upon God.

Schleiermacher sought to take full account of
the emerging historical research in his theological
program. By his time, the historical-critical method
was just beginning to open up a completely new
approach to the study of the Bible and the postbiblical tradition that challenged many received

notions regarding the origins of Israel and the church. Especially important was the idea of historical *development* in understanding the dynamic character of change in the formation and subsequent re-formation of the Christian religion from biblical times to the present day. Romanticism contributed to the new historical consciousness of the nineteenth century through its appreciation of individuality. In contrast to the disdain with which most Enlightenment thinkers held the historically given (or "positive") religious traditions, Schleiermacher argued that each one is an individual formation of the common essence of religion. Hence, a genuine feeling for individuality will not lead to rejection of what history has produced; rather, the appropriate attitude is the desire to cultivate each individual in its unique relation to the universe and to celebrate the diversity which the various individuals represent. In this fashion, Schleiermacher was a pioneer in appreciating religious plurality.

Schleiermacher came up with a method by which to discern the unique essence of a positive religion. It is to be found in the following four hallmarks: (1) stage of religious development, (2) type of religion, (3) originating event, and (4) central idea. Like Hume, Schleiermacher did not believe that monotheism was the earliest form of human religion. Instead, he claimed that it represents the highest stage in the evolutionary development of the religious consciousness. In addition to being monotheistic with respect to its stage of development, Christianity is an example of the *teleological* (oriented to an end or purpose) type of religion, wherein the relation to moral activity is crucial.[23] Its originating event is the ministry of Jesus, and its central idea is redemption from sin. The distinctiveness of Christianity lies in the fact that all religious affections are related to the redemption that Jesus makes possible. Jesus possessed an absolutely perfect consciousness of God, which was "a veritable existence of God in him."[24] Through participation in the power of his relation to God, Christians are enabled to overcome their own enfeebled God-consciousness. Christian doctrines give intellectual expression to this experience of redemption, just as Christian morals give practical expression to the active impulses of the redeemed God-consciousness.[25]

Christian theology "can only express God in his relation to us."[26] What Schleiermacher calls dogmatics (or systematic theology) is not a speculative enterprise, since it seeks only to describe the distinctive experience of Christian piety.[27] Hence, whatever attributes are predicated of God must not be understood "as denoting something special in God, but only something special in the manner in which the feeling of absolute dependence is to be related to him."[28] The doctrines of creation and preservation express the feeling of absolute dependence taken in abstraction from the antithesis of sin and grace. (Note that the doctrine of creation is not about how the world began!) The abstract consciousness of absolute dependence yields four attributes of God: eternity, omnipresence, omnipotence, and omniscience. The antithesis itself yields two pairs of attributes: the consciousness of sin is aware of God's holiness and justice, while the consciousness of grace reposes in God's wisdom and love. Apart from redemption through Christ, the Christian would never know that the absolute causality upon which the world depends is wise and loving. Hence, the affirmation of the goodness of creation belongs to the consciousness of redemption. The important thing to notice here is that there is no single locus for the doctrine of God in Schleiermacher's dogmatics since the attributes are spread throughout the entire system. Here is a parallel with Calvin, who also had no single doctrinal locus for God in his *Institutes* but divided his treatment into the twofold knowledge of God the creator and God the redeemer.

The antispeculative character of Schleiermacher's theology led him to relegate his treatment of trinitarian doctrine to an appendix in his systematic statement of Christian doctrine. As classically formulated, this doctrine is not an expression of the Christian religious self-consciousness.

> We have only to do with the God-consciousness given in our self-consciousness along with our consciousness of the world; hence we have no formula for the being of God in himself as distinct from the being of God in the world, and should have to borrow any such formula from speculation, and so prove ourselves disloyal to the character of the discipline at which we are working.[29]

Schleiermacher was fully persuaded that Christian faith in Christ and the redemption accomplished through him would remain unaltered if Christians made no claim to know something about God's being apart from God's relation to the world: "the main pivots of the ecclesiastical doctrine—the being of God in Christ and in the Christian Church—are independent of the doctrine of the Trinity."[30] He questioned the classical doctrine's exegetical foundation in the Bible and pointed out that this issue had already been raised during the Reformation. He thus called for a serious reconsideration of the alternative Sabellian or modalist doctrine, which had been rejected in the patristic period.

God as Absolute Spirit

A robust speculative reinterpretation of the Trinity was given by G. W. F. Hegel (1770–1831). Hegel represents the third great option for modern theology next to Kant and Schleiermacher. He agreed with Kant's critique of classical metaphysics, but he did not share Kant's strictures upon the limits of reason. For Hegel, God is not a mere postulate of the practical reason. The task for the philosophy of religion is to demonstrate the rational necessity of the content of religious faith. With respect to Schleiermacher, Hegel had nothing but disdain for a view of religion as feeling which, he thought, debased the human being by its exclusion of reason. Theology is not distinct from philosophy, as Schleiermacher believed; rather, theology is that part of philosophy that has to do with the knowledge of God. Moreover, if absolute dependence were truly the essence of religion, then a dog would be the best Christian! In stark contrast, Hegel affirmed that the human being finds its apotheosis in the feeling of freedom. Human history is the struggle to realize ever greater forms of freedom.

The church's dogmatic tradition teaches about God in the religious form of the representation (*Vorstellung*), which is an imaginative picture-language. The task for the philosophy of religion is to translate the timeless truth underlying the ecclesial dogma into the precise language of the concept (*Begriff*), thereby freeing it from its inadequate representational form. Only then can it be grasped in its real significance as expressing the highest knowledge about God. For Hegel, the historical, dogmatic form of Christianity has to be overcome (*aufgehoben*) through philosophy. In other words, it has to be negated in order that its own enduring truth may be thought. In pushing beyond the representation to the concept, philosophy is higher than religion. Yet, precisely thereby, philosophy also renders an apologetic service in showing that Christianity is "the absolute religion" because in it alone has been revealed the necessary truth that God is "spirit."

Spirit (*Geist*) is a dynamic concept. It implies an outgoing movement from itself to that which is other, only to return to itself again. This means that God is necessarily revelatory. The affirmation that God is spirit does not refer, as in the church's theology, only to the third person of the Trinity. Hegel's point is that God *is* spirit. Classical metaphysics applied the category "substance" to God, but Hegel insisted that the ultimate reality is "subject": "everything depends on comprehending and expressing the true as *subject* no less than as *substance*."[31] Moreover, spirit can only be known by spirit (Rom. 8:15-16, 26-27; John 4:23-24).[32] Herein is the point of identity between God and humanity. Human spirit is finite whereas the divine spirit is infinite. The infinite spirit comes to consciousness of itself through the finite spirit's knowledge of it. Nature is the state of spirit's estrangement from itself. The emergence of humanity signifies the breakthrough of spirit into nature. Here spirit attains three forms: "subjective" spirit in the psychology of individual persons, "objective" spirit in the legal and political institutions of society, and "absolute" spirit in art, religion, and philosophy. Through this developmental history of the human spirit, the divine spirit becomes conscious of itself as "Absolute Spirit." The religious relation of the human to God is, therefore, the expression of God's own self-relatedness.

In Hegel's speculative recasting of it, the profound truth about God disclosed in the doctrine of the Trinity is that the infinite is not separate from the finite but must be realized or actualized in it and through it. The implicit or essential unity of the divine-human relationship has been made explicit or actual in the historical fact of the incarnation of Christ. Hence, the history of both God and humanity has undergone change. God emptied himself into the finite, thereby negating himself as "other" than the world. The Father died in the incarnation and crucifixion of the Son. This leads to the emergence of Absolute Spirit, in which the estrangement between the finite and the infinite is reconciled. History is necessary for the fulfillment of this dialectical process of estrangement, nega-tion, and reconciliation of infinite spirit and finite spirit. As the infinite, God both negates and con-summates finitude.

The problem with traditional theology, as Hegel saw it, is that it represents God as a transcendent being with full self-consciousness apart from his self-divestment in the world. But, in Hegel's rein-terpretation of trinitarian theology, God requires the world in order to become Absolute Spirit. But the world is not, for that reason, something exter-nal to God. As one writer explains, "The divine object exists strictly for its own sake and has no relation to anything external and totally alien to itself; this is why it is called 'absolute'. It surely does have relations, but these are all internal, being constituted by God's creation of the world as the dimension of otherness within the divine pleni-tude."[33] God is the rational structure of reality, but this structure is dynamic and, hence, historical.

In Hegel's philosophy, reason is historical and history is rational. Indeed, human history itself is the revelation of God. Not only did Hegel propose a new way to understand God that brought history into the divine being, but he also provided a great stimulus to historical research in the nineteenth century on account of his belief that the human spirit has a history (in the work of disciples like F. C. Baur). Furthermore, for some theologians, his ideas would provide a compelling philosophical framework within which to speak anew of God's saving acts in history after the historical-critical study of the Bible had appeared to demolish this notion altogether (one such contemporary theologian is Wolfhart Pannenberg).

The Critique of Religion

Hegel's philosophy received a radical recasting at the hands of his left-wing disciples, Ludwig Feuerbach (1804–1872) and Karl Marx (1818–1883). They turned the master on his head by substituting humanity for God as the subject of the process of self-alienation and reconciliation with itself. Feuerbach believed that what people call God is really humanity alienated from its own true essence. In theology, humanity projects its alienated self into objective reality and arrives at the illusory concept of God. God is humanity's relinquished self:

> The divine being is nothing else than the human being or, rather, the human nature purified, freed from the limits of the individual man, made objective, that is, contemplated and revered as another, a distinct being. All the attributes of the divine nature are, therefore, attributes of the human nature. . . . God is the idea of the species as an individual.[34]

Anthropology is thus the key to theology. In order for alienated humanity to be reconciled to itself, theology must be overcome and the qualities that have traditionally been attributed to God must be reclaimed as expressing the essence of human nature.

Central to Christianity has been the affirmation that "God is love" (1 John 4:8). But this affirmation, correctly understood, is an indication that what is most important about humanity is love for our neighbor. Hence, what has hitherto been deemed the predicate ("God is *love*") must now be converted into the subject ("*love* is divine"). God must be denied for the sake of an authentic humanity.

> Who, then, is our Saviour and Redeemer? God or Love? . . . As God has renounced himself out of love, so we, out of love, should renounce God; for if we do not sacrifice God to love, we sacrifice love to God, and, in spite of the predicate of love, we have the God—the evil being—of religious fanaticism.[35]

Once humanity's alienation from the best qualities of its own nature has been overcome through the denial of theism, a new humanism will emerge in which the true purpose of the gospel's message about neighbor-love will find its genuine fulfillment.

Marx took Feuerbach's reversal of Hegel as his starting point, since he affirmed that the critique of religion is foundational to the critique of society itself. But Marx believed that Feuerbach did not go far enough. Feuerbach treated humanity as though it had an abstract essence, whereas Marx believed that human life is always concretely situated in a particular society with a definite history. For Marx, the economic forces of history determine human consciousness in each age. The ideas of a culture, including its religious beliefs, are the ideological superstructure that serves both to conceal and to justify the dominant economic relations:

> Does it require deep intuition to comprehend that man's ideas, views and conceptions, in one word, man's consciousness, changes with every change in the conditions of his material existence, in his social relations and in his social life? What else does the history of ideas prove, than that intellectual production changes its character in proportion as material production is changed? The ruling ideas of each age have ever been the ideas of its ruling class.[36]

"Law, morality, religion" are, to the oppressed worker struggling under the conditions of modern capitalism, "so many bourgeois prejudices, behind which lurk just as many bourgeois interests."[37] Hence, for Marx, the critique of religion must proceed to the analysis and overthrow of the economic conditions that generate the need for the illusions of religion.

Charles Darwin (1809–1882), though not himself a theologian or philosopher, carried forward the challenge of modern science to the traditional Christian view through his evolutionary theory of human origins. This theory presupposed that geological time extends into a remote past, since only such a long span of time can account for the observable features of the earth and for the remains of the fossil record. On the basis of the biblical genealogies, Bishop Ussher (1581–1656) had calculated the date of creation to be 4004 B.C.E. But, according to Darwin's view, the evolution of the human race out of earlier species was a process that took millions of years. Darwin's theory took into account that certain animal species have become extinct. Furthermore, it proposed that species are not immutable. They change over the course of generations in order to adapt themselves to the shifting conditions of their environments. This is the principle of natural selection. Those animals that successfully adapt to these changes survive to breed and they hand down their traits to their offspring. Darwin's theory managed to put all of the existing evidence into a coherent developmental scheme. Unlike the earlier science of the eighteenth century, Darwin introduced the idea of history into nature itself. The challenge to religion lay not only in the questioning of the Genesis account of creation but also in the erasure of the radical dichotomy between humanity and other species (cf. Eccles. 3:18-21). Darwin's account of the development of species also made it more difficult to argue for the existence of God on the basis of evidences of design, since his theory implied that the evolutionary process was random and haphazard in a way that excluded the notion of teleology.[38]

Sigmund Freud (1856–1939), the pioneer of psychoanalysis, built upon Darwin's views and added his own psychoanalytic critique of religious belief. According to Freud, the human being is driven by unconscious drives and instincts, especially sexuality and aggression. But the demands of civilization require a renunciation of these instinctual drives for the sake of social cohesion. The psychic mechanism by which these drives are sublimated into socially acceptable pursuits is called repression. The conscious mind is unaware of its own repressed desires, but they find expression in other ways. Neurosis, which is a disturbance of the mental and emotional life of the individual, is the price we pay for civilization. Freud interpreted religious belief as analogous to a neurosis. Belief in God is a compensation for the renunciations required of us by socialization into adulthood. The ambivalence of the child toward the father is sublimated into the idea of God. The father is necessary for the survival of the child and, at the same time, represents the principle of resistance to the fulfillment of its wishes. Through belief in God, we are consoled about the sacrifice of our instinctual desires and are assured of survival in the face of our helplessness with respect to the impersonal forces of nature.[39]

As the nineteenth century came to a close, Ernst Troeltsch (1865–1923) was engaged in reflecting upon the implications of "historicism" for Christianity and Western civilization. The consistent application of the historical-critical method to the

Bible had resulted in a fundamental shift in the interpretation of the scriptures. Whereas classical theologians had approached the Bible with the presupposition of its divine inspiration, modern historical scholars looked upon it as reflecting the diverse (and sometimes even conflicting) theological perspectives of its various human authors. Moreover, the "history of religions school" (*religionsgeschichtliche Schule*) had begun to point out parallels between certain biblical ideas and the religious notions of other cultures in the ancient Near East and the Greco-Roman world. Hence, cherished beliefs about the utter uniqueness of biblical revelation were threatened by the thoroughgoing historicist perspective, which had come to dominate the academic study of the Bible. In Troeltsch's assessment, the historical method issues in the acknowledgment of historical and cultural relativity in the spheres of religion and morality. As a result, he eventually distanced himself from the evolutionary schemes of religious development made famous by Schleiermacher and Hegel. He rejected the idea that Christianity—or any religion, for that matter—could claim to be "the absolute religion." Christianity is the religion of European civilization that emerged at the intersection of three cultures: Hebrew, Greek, and Latin. From this relativistic standpoint, Christians should meet representatives of the other world religions (for example, Buddhism and Hinduism) as equals, and the aims of Christian missionary activity should be rethought completely.[40]

The modern era brought a new set of challenges to the agenda of theology. For many persons, however, it was no longer possible to be a Christian or to believe in God at all after the Enlightenment had carried out its work of criticism. Friedrich Nietzsche (1844–1900) gave poignant expression to the post-Christian sensibility of Western culture when he prophesied "the death of God."[41] Some theologians in the twentieth century continued and refined the novel approaches to the question of God initiated in the eighteenth and nineteenth centuries; others criticized them in order to place faith in God on a new footing altogether after the theistic assumptions of Christendom could no longer be taken for granted. Hence, the twentieth century has to be seen in its relations of both continuity and discontinuity with what preceded it.

8

The Twentieth Century

Karl Barth (1886–1968) was the most important theologian of the twentieth century. He turned aside from the direction set for theology by the nineteenth century and sought to revive a distinctively "Reformation" approach to the question of the knowledge of God. He believed that Protestant theology had lost its identity through its various apologetic strategies to find a hearing for itself in the modern world. Schleiermacher was the especial target of Barth's criticism, but Barth also held Schleiermacher in high esteem and regarded him as the greatest theologian since the Reformation. Because these two giants of modern theology both stood in the Reformed tradition, the contrast between them with respect to theological method and substance is illustrative of the interpretive question involved in appropriating a medieval tradition after the Enlightenment. In spite of Barth's claim to leap over the nineteenth century in order to recover the Reformation heritage, his theology is just as thoroughly modern as Schleiermacher's. Since John Calvin never had to face the distinctive challenges to which Barth and Schleiermacher were forced to respond, his heirs are poised between two brilliant alternatives for construing his legacy in the modern world.

Karl Barth's Christocentrism

Barth rejected the category *religion* and, instead, sought to place theology firmly on its own foundation by means of a strong doctrine of revelation. Whereas Schleiermacher had interpreted Christian faith as a historically particular modification of the essence of religion, Barth feared that starting with the religious subject led necessarily to the complete reduction of theology into anthropology, as evident in the thought of Ludwig Feuerbach. Actually, Barth did not disagree with Feuerbach on his own terms; indeed, he was more than willing to endorse the radical critiques of religion as illusion and ideology advanced by the enemies of theology. But for Barth, revelation is the overcoming of human religion by God. In Barth's equation, religion is the effort of human beings to justify themselves by works, whereas revelation is God's grace to human beings. Ironically, then, for Barth faith in the gospel is thus antithetical to religion. Note the contrast with Calvin's use of terminology: Calvin had spoken of faith as the restoration of true religion or piety. Barth would allow for only a highly qualified use of the term *religion* with reference to Christianity. On the one hand, Christianity is a religion and, as such, is subject to the critique of it by revelation. On the other hand, Christianity may be said to be "the true religion" on the basis of revelation alone, just as a sinner may be said to be righteous through faith alone.[1]

Furthermore, Barth rejected every form of natural theology, and he believed that this was the great temptation besetting theology in every age. By *natural theology*, Barth did not mean simply arguments for the existence of God, such as we find in Thomas Aquinas. Although both Immanuel Kant and Friedrich Schleiermacher had understood themselves to have sought alternatives to natural theology, Barth considered their efforts to place theological affirmations in relation to either the moral or religious experience of the human subject as falling under his critique. Hence, what Barth meant by *natural theology* is broader than what the term traditionally signified. Schleiermacher would certainly have been surprised to find that he was guilty of it! But the question of natural theology also led to a controversy between Barth and another Reformed theologian, Emil Brunner (1889–1966), regarding the status of natural theology in Calvin's theology. Brunner advocated for what he called a "Christian Natural Theology," by which he meant that God's revelation through creation can be seen again once faith in Christ has removed the blinders of sin from our eyes. Calvin had said virtually the same thing, but Barth was emphatic in his *Nein* to all forms of natural theology.[2] Here the crucial difference not only between Barth and Brunner but also between Barth and Calvin emerges: Barth worked with a strict "christocentrism" in his doctrine of revelation. Indeed,

Barth is the most radically christocentric theologian in the history of Christianity. In the classical tradition, natural theology was assumed to be not only philosophically legitimate but also biblically justified (for example, Rom. 1:19-20). After it had become philosophically problematic in the modern period, Barth also tried to argue that it stood in radical contradiction to God's revelation in Christ as the Bible bears witness to it. For Barth, we can't even know about the existence of God apart from the revelation in Christ. There is no "point of contact" (*Anknüpfungspunkt*) between the gospel and human reason or experience. God's revelation in Christ makes its own point of contact by establishing faith in itself. In this way, Barth secured the independence of theology from the entanglements with philosophy, thereby enabling theology to stand on its own feet. Theology has no other task than to listen obediently to God's Word in Christ.

In the early period of his "dialectical theology," Barth emphasized the theme of God's radical transcendence, which cannot be domesticated in any way by human culture, philosophy, or religion: "One can *not* speak of God simply by speaking of man in a loud voice."[3] His thought during this period was a response to the breakdown of modern civilization and the exposure of its illusions through World War I (1914–1918). During the 1930s, when the Nazis were coming to power in Germany, Barth's theology underwent a shift in emphasis. Whereas in the aftermath of the war

Barth had emphasized the otherness of God, he now qualified this assertion of God's transcendence with the affirmation of God's unique self-revelation in Jesus Christ. God, who is completely independent of any human claims and pretensions, has in sovereign freedom chosen to reveal himself once and for all in Christ. The good news of this revelation is that "God is for man."[4] Hence, the earlier emphasis upon divine judgment was replaced with the joyful note that Christ is Emmanuel, "God with us" (Matt. 1:23). Through the power of this theology, Barth gave leadership to the "Confessing Church" in Germany as it attempted to resist the infiltration of Nazi ideology into the Protestant churches.

Unlike Schleiermacher, who argued for a modalist interpretation of trinitarian doctrine and placed his discussion of it in an appendix to his dogmatics, Barth sought to revive trinitarianism and to make it the basis for his doctrine of revelation. He also reversed Schleiermacher's order by treating the Trinity at the beginning of his dogmatics: "God's Word is God himself in his revelation. For God reveals himself as the Lord and according to Scripture this signifies for the concept of revelation that God himself in unimpaired unity yet also in unimpaired distinction is Revealer, Revelation, and Revealedness."[5] In his self-revelation, God discloses himself to be personal. Indeed, God is the true person, whereas human beings are persons only by analogy. This is not the "analogy of being" one finds in natural theology, but the "analogy of faith" (Rom. 12:6, according to the Greek text). God simply is who he reveals himself to be. There is no "hidden" God behind his revelation in Jesus Christ, since "God is who he is in the act of his revelation."[6]

Barth's radical christocentrism, which restricts knowledge of God solely to the revelation in Christ, is coupled with a revision in the doctrine of election. Barth rejected Calvin's doctrine of double predestination. For him, a theologian who attends only to God's Word in Christ has no grounds for affirming any other decree of God than that of God's will for the salvation of humanity. The pivotal verse for the reinterpretation of election is Ephesians 1:4: "[God] chose us in Jesus Christ before the foundation of the world." In Barth's exegesis, the word "us" refers to all of humanity. The consequence is that Barth's epistemological christocentrism brings with it a soteriological universalism since the content of the gospel is nothing other than the message that God is for humanity. The difference between Christians and non-Christians is not that the former are saved while the latter are damned; rather, Christians already know that they are saved whereas non-Christians do not yet know this great news! Barth criticized Calvin for engaging in an illicit bit of natural theology when he propounded his doctrine of double predestination since this contradicts "the humanity of God" revealed in the gospel:

> It is when we look at Jesus Christ that we know decisively that God's deity does not exclude but includes his *humanity*. Would that Calvin had energetically pushed ahead on this point in his

Christology, his doctrine of God, his teaching about predestination, and then logically also in his ethics! His Geneva would then not have become such a gloomy affair.[7]

Like the Arminians who also rejected double predestination, Barth denied the doctrine of limited atonement. But unlike them, he retained the other emphases repudiated by them as well, namely, the depth of sin's corruption, unconditional election, irresistible grace, and perseverance of the saints. He thereby revised his own Reformed tradition at its most vulnerable point through his doctrine of the sovereignty of God's grace in Christ. In this way Barth had also developed his own brand of humanism—which was the burning concern of the antitheologians in the nineteenth century—on the basis of this theological objectivity in the doctrine of God's self-revelation in Jesus Christ.

Paul Tillich and Ultimate Concern

Whereas Barth was untroubled by modern atheism, Paul Tillich (1886–1965) was deeply concerned with it and attempted to address it on its own terms. He adapted his own Lutheran heritage to speak to the religious situation of the twentieth century, just as Barth had revised the Reformed tradition. Through a radical reinterpretation of Luther's doctrine of justification, Tillich believed he had found a way to make the authentic meaning of faith speak with a fresh voice. Tillich critiqued the intellectualistic, voluntaristic, and emotionalistic distortions of the meaning of faith in the history of Christianity that have obscured its true meaning. By contrast, faith is a centered act of the entire person and cannot be identified with merely the intellect, the will, or the emotions. Properly understood, "faith is the state of being ultimately concerned."[8]

Tillich intended this definition to be a contemporary translation of the great commandment, "You shall love the LORD your God with all your heart, and with all your soul, and with all your might" (Deut. 6:5). In his view, all persons live by faith, whether they know it or not. "The term 'ultimate concern' unites a subjective and an objective meaning: somebody is concerned about something he considers of concern. In this formal sense of faith as ultimate concern, every human being has faith."[9] The crucial issue is not whether we are ultimately concerned but what we are ultimately concerned about. The question to be posed is whether the object of our subjective ultimate concern is truly ultimate. In his *Large Catechism*, Luther had given this exposition of the first commandment:

> A god is that to which we look for all good and in which we find refuge in every time of need. To have a god is nothing else than to trust and believe him with our whole heart. As I have often said, the trust and faith of the heart alone make both God and an idol. If your faith and trust are right, then your God is the true God. On the other hand, if your trust is false and wrong, you have not the true God. For these two belong together, faith and God.[10]

In Tillich's recasting of Luther's point, idolatry is the elevation to ultimate concern of those things that are really penultimate. Since that about which we are ultimately concerned has to do with our being or nonbeing, God alone—as the power of being-itself—is the only proper object of faith.

Tillich was convinced that inadequate concepts of God have also led to the problem of modern atheism. God is not properly "a being" at all. To speak in this manner brings God into the subject-object correlation of finitude and makes God finite.

> The being of God is being-itself. The being of God cannot be understood as the existence of a being alongside others or above others. If God is *a* being, he is subject to the categories of finitude. . . . Even if he is called the "highest being" in the sense of the "most perfect" and the "most powerful" being, this situation is not changed. When applied to God, superlatives become diminutives. . . . Whenever infinite or unconditional power and meaning are attributed to the highest being, it has ceased to be a being and has become being-itself. Many confusions in the doctrine of God and many apologetic weaknesses could be avoided if God were understood first of all as being-itself or as the ground of being.[11]

Although some critics accused Tillich of atheism for his denial that God is a being, his meaning is not really all that different from what many classical theologians had said. As a consequence of this doctrine of God, Tillich denied that there can be a literal language for speaking about God.[12] All our language about God is symbolic. In response to the objection that he has made the language of theology "merely symbolic," Tillich answered that the criticism itself is symptomatic of the impoverishment of symbolic language in our technical scientific culture and betrays a lack of insight into the depth-dimension of human existence, which only religious symbols are capable of illuminating.

Like Schleiermacher, Tillich was critical of personalistic language for God. A personal God stands over-against us in an "I-Thou" relationship, but God as the ground of being is not separate from us. Tillich did not reject the religious use of personal terms altogether, but he was opposed to them when their symbolic character is forgotten and they are taken literally. He affirmed that, as persons, we must have a personal relationship to God, but that doesn't mean that God is a person.

> Being includes personal being; it does not deny it. The ground of being is the ground of personal being, not its negation. . . . Religiously speaking, this means that our encounter with the God who is a person includes the encounter with the God who is the ground of everything personal and as such not *a* person.[13]

In contrast to Schleiermacher, however, Tillich affirmed the necessity of trinitarian symbolism for the inner life of God. In this respect he saw himself as having a greater kinship with Hegel. Tillich criticized Schleiermacher for understanding the doctrine of the Trinity only in relation to Christology, whereas Hegel correctly grasped its import: "The living God is always the trinitarian God, even before Christology is possible. . . . He is not a dead oneness in himself, a dead identity, but he goes out and returns."[14] Even Unitarians, who reject the doctrine of the Trinity for christological reasons, are necessarily "trinitarian" insofar as they affirm the symbol of the living God.

In contrast to Barth, Tillich argued that every theology worth its salt always includes the task of apologetics or explaining and defending Christian faith in addition to the dogmatic task of determining the correct interpretation of the church's proclamation.[15] He developed a "method of correlation" through which he sought to make contact with the existential questions of modern persons and to reformulate the meaning of the gospel's proclamation in a way that it can be heard as providing an answer to these questions. He believed that that is how theology has historically operated. In the ancient world when the existential question was fate and mortality, the gospel was interpreted as providing an answer through the incarnation of the eternal *logos* (by Athanasius). In the medieval world when the terrified conscience trembled at the prospect of eternal damnation, the gospel was reformulated to assure sinners of their acceptance before a merciful God (by Luther). In the twentieth century, Tillich perceived that the question was meaninglessness and despair in the face of "the death of God." The threat of nonbeing no longer takes the form of death or guilt but appears in the

haunting sense that human existence has no ultimate meaning or purpose. Tillich asked: "Is there a
kind of faith which can exist together with doubt
and meaninglessness?"[16] He was persuaded that
Christian theology has to address this question
directly if the gospel is to be received as "good
news" for modern people. For Tillich, the way forward lay in grasping the crucial insight into faith
as ultimate concern:

> The fundamental symbol of our ultimate concern
> is God. It is always present in any act of faith,
> even if the act of faith includes the denial of God.
> Where there is ultimate concern, God can be
> denied only in the name of God. . . . Atheism,
> consequently, can only mean the attempt to
> remove any ultimate concern—to remain uncon-
> cerned about the meaning of one's existence.[17]

Just as Luther had affirmed the paradox that we are
justified and yet sinners, so Tillich sought to reformulate Luther's point by insisting that faith justifies even the person who is in the state of doubt
about God: "The Lutheran courage [to face the
threat of nonbeing] returns but not supported by
the faith in a judging and forgiving God."[18]

The Radical Faith of H. Richard Niebuhr

H. Richard Niebuhr (1894–1962) was greatly influenced by the historicism of Troeltsch. While
sharing many of Barth's criticisms of nineteenth-
century theology, Niebuhr stood in a line of continuity with the approaches of Kant and Schleiermacher and, as such, was very concerned about

the implications for moral life of religious faith in
God. Unlike Barth, Niebuhr did not think a christocentric doctrine of revelation was the only way
to preserve God's objectivity and transcendence.
Instead, he sought to clarify the meaning of radical faith in God or, as he called it, "radical
monotheism."

"Faith," for Niebuhr, is a double-sided concept:
it means both confidence and fidelity. Like Barth,
Niebuhr did not use the concept of religion as the
broader category for interpreting faith. With
Tillich, Niebuhr was convinced that all persons live
by faith. The phenomenon of faith is not restricted
to the religious sphere but is manifested in every
area of human life, including the scientific and the
political realms. The real issue today is not the conflict between one religion and another, nor is it the
struggle of religion with secularism. The crucial
issue, rather, is the choice between three forms of
faith: polytheism, henotheism, and radical monotheism. These terms, which are drawn from the
history of religion, are used by Niebuhr in a non-
mythological sense to indicate the various centers
of value around which we organize our lives. The
"gods" thus refer, not to supernatural beings, but to
"value-centers and objects of devotion."[19]

The henotheist has a social faith in a group, be
it family, tribe, nation, race, or civilization. Polytheism emerges when social faith has been disap-
pointed. Then the objects of loyalty and confidence
become diversified. As a rule, most persons are
practical polytheists, even if they pay lip service to

a monotheistic creed: "Sometimes they live for Jesus' God, sometimes for country and sometimes for Yale."[20] Radical monotheism is distinct from both henotheism and polytheism, since it refers "to no one reality among the many but to One beyond all the many, whence all the many derive their being, and by participation in which they exist." As he says:

> It is the confidence that whatever is, is good, because it exists as one thing among the many which all have their origin and their being, in the One—the principle of being which is also the principle of value. . . . Monotheism is less than radical if it makes a distinction between the principle of being and the principle of value; so that while all being is acknowledged as absolutely dependent for existence on the One, only some beings are valued as having worth for it; or if, speaking in religious language, the Creator and the God of grace are not identified.[21]

The counterpart to confidence in the principle of being as the principle of value is loyalty to the realm of being that is to be valued. Faith in God as the good creator of all things brings with it fidelity to God's good creation, which is inclusive of all things. Hence, "even enemies are entitled to loyalty as fellow citizens of the realm of being," since "my enemy is my companion in being" (Matt. 5:43-45).[22]

When measured according to the criterion of radical monotheism, the officially monotheistic religions are shown to be forms of henotheism.

Christians have been tempted to criticize Judaism as particularistic on account of its being the religion of a nation, but the struggle of monotheism with social henotheism has also appeared in Christianity, though in different forms. A church-centered form of henotheism has appeared in Catholicism, whereas in Protestantism it has taken a Christ-centered form. "No reformation remains reformed; no catholic church remains all-inclusive. The One beyond the many is confused again and again with one of the many."[23] In Niebuhr's historicist reframing of the meaning of revelation, Christians point to or "confess" those events in their history that have elicited radical faith. "Jesus represents the incarnation of radical faith," but Christians must not confuse the particularity of their history with the universality of the God revealed by Jesus.[24]

Niebuhr gave a distinctive interpretation of the ecumenical significance of trinitarianism. With respect to the criticism of Christianity as tritheistic, Niebuhr suggested "it seems nearer the truth to say that Christianity as a whole is more likely to be an association, loosely held together, of three Unitarian religions."[25] There has been the unitarianism of the Father. Arianism, monarchianism, deism, and "Unitarianism" in the denominational sense of the term are all examples of this type. These groups tend to worship the principle of being that is the cause of all things. God is the power of nature, but it is doubtful whether this power is good. The second type is unitarianism of the Son, for which God is the redeemer or the principle of value. Marcion and Barth exemplify this type. The deity is the God of human history and its salvation, but it is doubtful whether the good God is powerful. Then there is the unitarianism of the Spirit, such as one finds in mysticism, in revivals of religious enthusiasm, and in modern philosophy, where the creative human spirit is virtually deified. Each form of unitarianism is inadequate by itself and must be willing to receive criticism from the others. A trinitarian doctrine of God does not identify God with one function only as do the various forms of unitarianism. With this recasting of the problem of radical monotheism and trinitariansim, Niebuhr sought to bridge many of the differences and historic conflicts in Christianity.

New Challenges and Agendas

Process Theology. Process theology is the most original contribution to a philosophical approach to the question of God in the twentieth century. It is based on the philosophy of Alfred North Whitehead (1861–1947), which was subsequently refined in greater detail with respect to its theological implications by Charles Hartshorne (1897–2000). Whitehead proposed a metaphysics that starts from the presupposition that human experience is our best clue to the nature of reality as such. He believed that Kant, following Hume, worked with a restricted notion of experience as "sense experience." The great problem in modern philosophy was this reduction of experience to the deliverances of sense data, but this robbed the emotional, artistic, moral, and religious dimensions of our experience of cognitive significance. Modern scientific materialism is based on this philosophical mistake of substituting an abstraction for the full concreteness of experience. Kant's restriction of knowledge to the combination of concepts with sense data is based upon this mistake. Process philosophy is intended as an alternative solution to the problems and questions that led Kant to reject metaphysics as an illicit use of reason. By contrast, Whitehead distinguished two forms of experience: sense experience ("experience in the mode of presentational immediacy") and "felt" experience ("experience in the mode of causal efficacy"). According to his view, all reality is made up of "occasions of experience." An experience is constituted by its relations to what precedes it. Each moment of experience "prehends" or feels the past and integrates this inheritance with a new "initial aim" or purpose. This aim is always the introduction of novelty into the process of becoming. God is the metaphysical principle that selects the relevant possibility for each new moment of experience.

God is not to be conceived as an exception to the general metaphysical categories. This means that process thinkers employ a univocal use of the metaphysical categories with respect to God and the world. God, too, is constituted by relations to the world. The idea of God's aseity has no meaning in this framework since nothing exists apart from its relationships. God has "internal relations," that is, what happens in the world affects God. Process theology thus rejects the idea that God is immutable and impassible. Whitehead spoke of both a "primordial nature" in God, which is the eternal envisioning by God of the realm of possibility, and a "consequent nature" in God, which is the completion of the world in God's own experience. Hartshorne distinguished between God's "existence" and God's "actuality," the former referring to the unchanging abstract character of God and the latter referring to the concrete experience of God, which is new in each moment.[26] In process theology, "creativity" is the metaphysical ultimate; moreover, God and the world require one another. Whitehead explained: "Neither God, nor the World, reaches static completion. Both are in the grip of the ultimate metaphysical ground, the creative advance into novelty. Either of them, God and the World, is the instrument of novelty for the other."[27] The future is genuinely open for God since God does not have foreknowledge of future events. Moreover, God cannot exercise power unilaterally to bring about just any state of affairs. God's power is persuasive, not coercive. God is not omnipotent.

Process theology resembles Plato's vision in which God is the "demiurge" who brings order into the preexisting chaos. In both viewpoints, the world was not created by God "out of nothing." With reference to modern religious thought, process theology is an example of "panentheism" (literally, "all is in God"), which seeks the mean between the extremes of transcendence, as in deism, and of immanence, as in pantheism. God's being includes the world but is not exhausted by it.

For this reason, process theology also bears comparison with Hegel's theology of spirit. Moreover, both of these viewpoints are explicitly metaphysical ways of speaking about God.

Whitehead's philosophy is of interest to theologians for two main reasons: first, it offers a theistic metaphysics that takes full account of modern scientific knowledge; second, it proposes a new way to conceive of God that departs from the metaphysical assumptions of Greek philosophy with which classical Christian theology has operated.

For process theologians, the big mistake of classical theology was the uncritical adoption of the Greek philosophical assumptions about the nature of deity. Such ideas make it impossible to understand the Christian claim that God is personal and loving. Love, by definition, means the capacity to be affected by others. Whitehead wrote: "When the world accepted Christianity, Caesar conquered. . . . The brief Galilean vision of humility flickered throughout the ages, uncertainly. . . . The Church gave unto God the attributes which belonged exclusively to Caesar."[28] Hence, process theologians believe that Whitehead's metaphysics offers a conceptuality that makes sense of the central religious affirmations about the God known in Jesus.[29] They believe, moreover, that modern atheism is, in part, a reaction to classical theism's view of God, which teaches that God is the omnipotent determiner of all events. This view denies the reality of human freedom and the meaningfulness of human history.[30] Process theologians also dispute that it is possible to do theology apart from explicit attention to metaphysical issues since all theologians, even those who exclude metaphysics from their theological methods (for example, Schleiermacher and Barth), presuppose such concepts in their interpretations of Christian faith.[31]

Liberation theology. Liberation theology has worked at the concept of God mainly from the perspective of an ethical critique of traditional Christian theology as underwriting socioeconomic systems of domination and oppression. The inspiration for this movement came from the Peruvian Roman Catholic theologian, Gustavo Gutiérrez (b. 1928), whose ground-breaking book, *A Theology of Liberation*, was first published in English in 1971. Liberation theology articulates a perspective that focuses less on doctrine and more on *praxis,* that is, self-critical engagement on behalf of the poor and downtrodden people of the earth. Whereas modern theology in Europe and North America has been primarily concerned to address the plight of the nonbeliever, liberation theologians turn their attention to the nonperson, those who lack sufficient means to feed and clothe themselves. This theology represents a radical challenge to Western theology from the so-called third world, which continues to suffer under the impact of its colonial past. Liberation theologians retrieve the prophetic heritage of ancient Israel in which service of God is inextricably bound up with justice for the neighbor (Mic. 6:8; Isa. 58:6-7): "The God of Biblical revelation is known through interhuman justice. Where justice does not exist, God is not known."[32] In the

New Testament, Jesus is depicted as identifying with the poor and the lowly, feeding the hungry and pronouncing judgment upon the wealthy. Moreover, he renders this verdict upon his disciples who refuse their help to those in need: "As you did it not to one of the least of these . . . you did it not to me" (Matt. 25:45). In imitation of him, Christians must adopt the same posture by standing in solidarity with the oppressed against their oppressors.

Liberation theologians argue that the establishment of Christianity under Constantine led to the loss of its prophetic critique of societal injustice. During the era of Christendom, theology stood under the shadow of the ruling powers and thus allowed itself to become an "ideology" in Marx's sense of the word. These theologians affirm that Marx's method of critical social analysis can be disentangled from his sweeping view of all religion as "the opiate of the people." Liberation theology has undertaken to respond to Marx by demonstrating that the authentic meaning of the Bible *is* the message of God's liberation of the oppressed. Unlike a great deal of traditional Christian theology, which focused upon salvation in the afterlife, this theology is decidedly oriented toward a transformation of economic and political conditions in this life. Liberation theologians have used Marxist analysis to expose the social locations and ideological functions of other theologies that have perverted the gospel for the sake of legitimating conditions of oppression by teaching that patient suffering of this world's inequities will be rewarded in the life to come. Although liberation theology emerged in Latin America where the vast majority of the population lives in abject poverty, it has found a home in North America as well, where it has been adapted by oppressed minorities for the purpose of upholding the dignity of those persons who have to fight against racism, sexism, heterosexism, and other forms of oppression to which the dominant culture subjects them.

Black Theology. James H. Cone (b. 1938) began his reflections upon the theological implications of the African-American experience in the United States prior to the emergence of liberation theology. Indeed, he scolds white theologians for being more interested in conversing with the Latin American theologians half a world away than with the black theologians on the other side of town. Black theology poses a unique challenge to theology in the United States on account of the history of slavery. Ironically, the slaves first came to embrace the gospel through the instruction of their masters, for whom there was no contradiction between Christian faith and slavery. Indeed, the Bible explicitly teaches that slaves should obey their masters (Eph. 6:5-8; 1 Peter 2:18-21). On the basis of their belief in the divine inspiration of the scriptures, white Christians during the Civil War argued that slavery does not contradict God's will. But the slaves seized upon another strand of the Bible's teaching. Through the story of the exodus from Egypt, the slaves learned of God's concern for their liberation from bondage (Exod. 3:7-10). And in Christ "there is neither slave nor free" (Gal. 3:28). The hermeneutical problem of the Bible with respect to ethics was nowhere more acute than here.

Cone began his theological career heavily influenced by Karl Barth. He modified Barth's construal of the gospel's message that God is for humanity by insisting that God is for *oppressed* humanity. In the meantime, his thought has moved away from Barth's method with respect to two central issues: the Bible and Christology. While Cone still takes the Bible seriously, it is no longer the sole repository of God's truth.

> I still regard the Bible as an important source of my theological reflections, but not the starting point. The black experience and the Bible together in dialectical tension serve as my point of departure. . . . The order is significant. I am *black* first—and everything else comes after that. This means that I read the Bible through the lens of a black tradition of struggle and not as the objective Word of God. The Bible therefore is one witness to God's empowering presence in human affairs, along with other important testimonies. The other testimonies include sacred documents of the African-American experience. . . .[33]

Part of this shift in his thinking is the result of acknowledging that the Bible does not speak unambiguously for the liberation of the oppressed. With respect to Christology, Cone continues to think that theological reflection upon Jesus is important, but this is not the Christ "of Nicea and Chalcedon, nor of Luther, Calvin, and Barth." He explains: "No longer can I do theology as if Jesus is God's *sole* revelation.

Rather he is an important revelatory event among many."[34] From Barth's perspective, Cone has committed the cardinal sin of natural theology. But for Cone, "the western theological tradition transmitted from Augustine to Barth" is not immediately applicable to the situation of black people "because our experience is different" from "that of my white colleagues."[35] Here the term *experience* takes on a much more specific, particular, and concrete meaning than it does in previous theologies that spoke abstractly of a religious dimension of common human experience (as in Schleiermacher and Tillich).

Feminist Theology. Feminist theology stands in this line of an ethical critique of traditional theology. Feminists point to the patriarchal and sexist character of the Christian tradition. To this day, the Eastern Orthodox and the Roman Catholics deny ordination to women on the grounds that Christ was male and, therefore, his priestly representatives must be men. Once again, the hermeneutical problem of the Bible has taken center stage. The Bible clearly teaches the subordination of women to men (1 Cor. 11:2, 7-9; 14:34-35; Eph. 5:22-24; 1 Tim. 2:11-15; 1 Peter 3:1-6). If the Bible is believed to be the written Word of God, then patriarchal social arrangements are divinely sanctioned. But here, too, there is another biblical motif that is difficult to reconcile with its exhortation that women should be subordinate to men: in Christ "there is neither male nor female" (Gal. 3:28).

Feminist theologians have critiqued the language about God found in the Bible and the church's tradition as "gendered discourse." The predominant use of masculine pronouns (*he* and *his*) as well as male images (*lord, father, king*) are not neutral with respect to their political and social implications. As Mary Daly (b. 1928) argued, "If God is male, then the male is God."[36] Nonetheless, feminist exegetes have pointed to a neglected dimension of the biblical heritage where female imagery is invoked to describe God (Isa. 42:14b; 46:3-4; 49:15; 66:13). Feminist theologians have also lifted up the biblical idea of the divine wisdom as a personification of God (for example, Prov. 8; 1 Cor. 1:24) since, in both Hebrew and Greek, *wisdom* is a feminine noun. Others have explored the theological implications of employing alternative metaphors to those found in the dominant tradition. Examples are the world as God's body and God as mother, lover, and friend.[37] And feminist historians have worked to retrieve the mystical tradition of Christianity in which women played such a large role (for example, Julian of Norwich).

Trinitarianism has been a double-edged sword for feminist theologians. Some have made a creative use of the idea of intra-trinitarian relations in God as exemplifying the essential relationality of God.[38] But when others have proposed revising the trinitarian formula to "Creator, Christ, and Spirit," objections have been raised by critics who insist that "Father, Son, and Spirit" is a divinely revealed name that cannot be replaced in modalist fashion by listing God's functions.[39] A few feminist theologians have left the Christian church altogether on the grounds that it is hopelessly patriarchal, and they have adopted the label "post-Christian" to describe their position.[40] But like Black theologians who have had to work against the legacy of slavery and the church's complicity with it, Christian feminists attempt to disentangle the liberating message of the gospel from the church's sexist past. For both groups, the Bible and the church's tradition are highly ambiguous and need to be sifted according to the norm of God's will for justice on behalf of all persons.

Moltmann's Trinitarianism. Recent theology has witnessed a revival of interest in trinitarianism. Aside from Barth's influence, the German Jesuit Karl Rahner (1904–1984) made an important contribution to this revival of trinitarian theology with his famous axiom: "The Trinity in the history and economy of salvation is the immanent Trinity."[41] Nevertheless, Jürgen Moltmann (b. 1926) has accused both Barth and Rahner of modalism. Whereas the ancient church had identified God as "the supreme substance," modern theology has defined God as "the absolute subject." Barth interpreted the trinitarian persons as three "modes of being" in God, and Rahner spoke of them as God's three "modes of presence" to us.[42] Both theologians, according to Moltmann, secured the divine unity in God's sovereignty, which means that they viewed God as a single self-identical subject:

> It is of decisive importance for the doctrine of God whether we start from the Trinity in order to understand the sovereignty of God as the sovereignty of the Father, the Son and the Spirit, or whether we think in the reverse direction, pro-

ceeding from the sovereignty of God in order to secure this as being the sovereignty of the One God by means of the doctrine of the Trinity.[43]

For this reason, these theologies are "monotheistic" and, as such, not truly trinitarian. Here we witness a Christian theologian explicitly repudiating the idea that the Christian doctrine of God is monotheistic. Modalism and monotheism are virtually equated by Moltmann. Furthermore, for him, the term *monotheism* is politically charged with all sorts of negative connotations. In his view, the apologists' acceptance of philosophical monotheism is what made it possible for Christianity to become the world religion of the Roman empire. He takes theocratic Islam as the best example of the consistent application of monotheism to politics. Monotheism is "an uncommonly seductive religious-political ideology."[44] Moltmann thus intends his criticism of monotheism to lend support to liberation and feminist theologies in their fight against hegemonic or oppressive systems of identity in which everything different is reduced to more of the same.

Yet Moltmann does not accept the opposite term *tritheism* to describe his viewpoint.[45] Instead, he calls his proposal a "social doctrine" of the Trinity, which begins "with the special Christian tradition of the history of Jesus the Son" and moves on from there "to develop a historical doctrine of the Trinity." The unity of God is a "tri-unity" of three persons in their mutual relations and interpenetration of one another. Moltmann retrieves the idea of *perichoresis* or *circumincessio* from John of Damascus: "this concept grasps the circulatory character of the eternal divine life. . . . By virtue of their eternal love they live in one another to such an extent, and dwell in one another to such an extent, that they are one."[46] Origin, too, had spoken of the unity of the three persons as their unity in love. Moltmann praises Origen, moreover, for his willingness to speak of the divine suffering: "Origen . . . talks about a divine passion which Christ suffers for us, and at the same time points to a divine passion between the Father and the Son in the Trinity."[47] In this way, Moltmann shares the critique of the classical tradition's insistence upon the divine impassibility given by the process theologians. But in his view, only a full-blown doctrine of God as Trinity can render the claim of God's love coherent. "For we *can* only talk about God's suffering in trinitarian terms. In monotheism it is impossible."[48]

Kaufman: Creativity as God. Moltmann's critique of monotheism is the polar opposite of Niebuhr's recommendation of it as the appropriate way in which to understand biblical faith in God. Niebuhr's student, Gordon Kaufman (b. 1925), has taken the tradition of his mentor a step further. Like Niebuhr, Kaufman is a historicist who believes that all our knowledge is historically and culturally relative and, as such, cannot be absolutized. Like Kant, Kaufman is deeply concerned about the moral implications of theistic faith. Yet, like Feuerbach, he believes that theology is an act of human imaginative construction of the symbol "God." In this respect, Kaufman differentiates himself from a view of theology as

based in God's revelation (Barth) or as a hemeneu-
tical or interpretive activity in which the timeless
message of scripture is translated into contemporary concepts (Tillich and Rudolf Bultmann). But he
also distances himself from Niebuhr's rather "soft"
claim for revelation, which is of a piece with
Niebuhr's "confessional" approach to how God has
acted in our history as Christians. Instead, Kaufman
adopts an explicitly "pragmatic" criterion for criti-
cizing and evaluating the significance of theological symbolism: does it enable us to live in the world
humanely? He believes that humans create imaginative world-pictures that orient human life. For
Christians, God is the central symbol that organizes
and brings into sharp focus the various values and
commitments of living as a Christian. One can see
the resemblance to Kant, who spoke of God as a
"regulative" idea. In Kaufman's view, theology's
task consists in the criticism and reconstruction of
the symbol or concept of God. He wants theologians to ask how this particular concept came to be
constructed by the human imagination and what
functions it serves:

> The notion of God is one of the most complexly
> dialectical of all human ideas. On the one hand, it
> is clearly *our* idea: we humans created it; we
> shaped and refined it in the course of history; and
> we continue to criticize and reconstruct it in our
> prophetic visions and our theologies. On the other
> hand, this is the idea of that which is beyond the
> reach of our highest thought, our loftiest aspiration,
> our most profound insight, our deepest intuition; it
> is in fact a *limiting idea,* an idea which cannot be

> thought simply or directly but only indirectly as
> that which limits, relativizes, calls into question, all
> that we are and do, experience and think.[49]

This symbol functions to relativize and to human-
ize. On the one hand, it prevents us from absolu-
tizing ourselves, our values and perspectives,
thereby keeping us humble: "our understanding of
God is closely interconnected with and dependent
upon the sharply contrasting notion of idols:
without the notion of idolatry we could not make
clear to ourselves what we mean by 'God.'"[50] On
the other hand, this symbol opens us to embrace a
genuinely humane mode of existence constituted
by love for the neighbor and care for the natural
world. "'God' is the name, thus, to which we can
give ourselves and our lives without reservation,
the proper object of our unqualified devotion, that
in terms of which human life in the world can
most properly be oriented."[51]

Initially, Kaufman defended the view that moral
agency can only be sustained in the long run by
means of a personalistic concept of God. But as his
thinking became increasingly concerned about the
ecological crisis, this aspect of his theology underwent revision, and he came to believe that the
anthropomorphism (attributing human characteristics to God) and personalism of Christian theism is
anthropocentric or human-centered. Human beings
need to see themselves not simply as historical
beings but also as biological beings. Hence, he
coined the description "bio-historical" to capture
this dual emphasis.[52] In place of the traditional con-

cepts of God as creator and lord of history, Kaufman has proposed that the referent of theistic symbolism now be understood as "serendipitous creativity." The adjective *serendipitous* expresses the surprising, unexpected, and inexplicable character of the fact that we find ourselves in the universe at all, that we humans are the products of processes of biological evolution and historical development that have brought us into being and of which we are the beneficiaries. The shift from "creator" to "creativity" reflects Kaufman's conviction that the traditional biblical imagery of God as a personal agent who created and rules the world is dualistic. This judgment is initially surprising when one remembers the struggle of the church's monotheism against the ancient forms of dualism. By this, however, he means that the tradition operated with "a fundamental duality in reality, a cleavage between God (the source of all that is) and God's creation (the world and all its contents)."[53] Yet such a model goes against the grain of our naturalistic and ecological perspective wherein all of reality is seen as a unity. God cannot be viewed as standing "outside" this interdependent web of natural and historical relationships.[54] "*God*, I now propose, is to be understood as the underlying reality (whatever it may be)—the ultimate mystery—expressing itself throughout the universe and thus also in this evolutionary-historical trajectory (of particular interest to us humans) which has produced humankind."[55]

Although Kaufman acknowledges his own Christian perspective as informing what he does, he insists that we cannot "continue to live and think simply in the limited terms which our much too parochial traditions have bequeathed to us." Hence, he identifies himself as a Christian theologian who "has begun to glimpse something of the richness and importance of the world beyond the West, and beyond Christian frameworks. . . ."[56] In response to those who point to the negative political and social effects whenever the church absolutized its own faith in God, Kaufman answers that the proper meaning (or function) of the symbol "God" is the best antidote:

> Whatever may be the dangers of the image/concept "God," it remains (at least in Western cultures) our most profound and comprehensive symbol, particularly with respect to its powers to draw all that we humans know or experience or can imagine together into an all-inclusive yet open and thoroughly differentiated Whole. . . . Theocentric symbolism, when rightly understood and interpreted, provides a point of reference in terms of which the ethnocentrism of its own bearer can be discerned and criticized; beyond this, it supplies a framework of orientation for human life which can overcome the anthropocentrism which we today see to be so destructive of the ecological web of life. It is the presence of this self-critical, and potentially self-correcting, principle at the very heart of this frame of orientation, and this alone, that can justify universalistic claims made in its behalf.[57]

Like Niebuhr, Kaufman has thus combined a radically monotheistic faith with a thoroughgoing historical and cultural relativism.

Gustafson's Theocentrism. Another of Niebuhr's students, James M. Gustafson (b. 1925), has also been concerned to develop a theological framework that can embrace the insights of historical and cultural relativism. Gustafson acknowledges that theology works within the context of a historic monotheistic tradition, but theologians must be self-critical and not claim to know more about God than is warranted by the evidence. Gustafson thinks that theologies based on revelation as well as natural theologies have claimed to know too much about God. Theology is based in ordinary human experiences and is primarily a practical enterprise, "an effort to make sense out of a very broad range of human experiences, to find some meaning in them and for them that enables persons to live and to act in coherent ways." It is "a way of construing the world" that reflects "an intention to relate to all things in a manner appropriate to their *relations* to God."[58]

Gustafson has issued a prophetic denunciation of the pernicious anthropocentrism he perceives to have infected the Western traditions of theology and ethics. The problem is that the human being has become "the measure of all things"—the ultimate center of value and the final point of reference for religion and morality. This anthropocentrism is at odds not only with the biblical critique of idolatry but also with the modern scientific understanding of humanity's place in the cosmos. The result is that we have "a Ptolemaic religion in a Copernican universe."[59] Gustafson acknowledges that there have been countervailing tendencies in the biblical and

Christian traditions and, through a selective retrieval of these "theocentric" strands, he has proposed one of the most radical alternatives to anthropocentrism. Specifically, he locates himself in the tradition of John Calvin, wherein the chief end of the human being is to serve God. Yet Gustafson is careful not to claim an identity between his position and Calvin's. Gustafson calls his development of Calvin's tradition "a Reformed theology, of sorts" on account of the many aspects of traditional Christian theology he discards in the light of what the sciences teach.[60] Gustafson criticizes modern theologians for not taking with complete seriousness the results of the modern sciences in rethinking traditional assumptions about God and humanity. He singles out Tillich and Moltmann as examples.[61] Although these theologians do not reject scientific explanations of the development of our planet and of our species, they continue to perpetuate the view that the human being and its fulfillment are the center of God's concerns. Gustafson calls for a displacement of humanity from the center of things. Christianity's preoccupation with human salvation places God in the service of human beings. Calvin's belief that concern with human salvation must be subordinated to the service of God can correct the tradition's soteriological focus.

Even the Reformed tradition, however, is guilty of anthropocentrism.[62] Unlike Calvin, Gustafson does away with the notion of God's special providence according to which all things are governed by God's intentions for the salvation of individual persons. In Gustafson's view, moreover, there is no life after death that can serve as a consolation for the miseries and injustices suffered by faithful persons. Gustafson criticizes the anthropomorphism of the classical doctrine of God, including Calvin's version of it. God does not have "intentions" as persons do, though God can be said to have "purposes" that may be discerned and in relation to which religious and moral life may be organized.[63] Gustafson appeals to the other strand in Calvin's thinking about God, which placed him in the vicinity of the Stoics: "nature is God."[64] Not surprisingly, Gustafson also appreciates Schleiermacher's appropriation of Spinoza's pantheism.

Like Calvin and Schleiermacher, Gustafson places a great deal of emphasis upon piety understood as the affections of religious and moral life. He prefers the word *piety* to *faith* since the former does not have the connotation of belief, and it does not mislead persons into trusting that fidelity to God issues in the good as they understand it. Piety involves consent to the divine governance, as this is discerned in the patterns and processes of interdependence in the world. The affections of piety are evoked by the various powers bearing down upon us and sustaining us as these are encountered in nature, history, society, culture, and the self. Theology construes these experiences with reference to an ultimate "Other" (God) that bears down upon us and sustains us in and through these "others." Theocentric piety is characterized by six affective "senses": a sense of dependence, gratitude, obligation, remorse or repentance, possibility, and direction. On the basis of these affections, theology is able to retrieve the symbols of God as creator, sustainer, governor, judge, and redeemer. "'God' refers to the power that bears down upon us, sustains us, sets an ordering of relationships, provides conditions of possibility for human activity and even a sense of direction."[65] The practical moral question from a theocentric perspective is: "What is God enabling and requiring us to be and to do?" The most general answer is: "We are to relate ourselves and all things in a manner appropriate to their relations to God."[66] For Gustafson, the Bible narrates the experiences of a people of theocentric piety as they sought to discern God's purposes in their various historical contexts. "Jesus incarnates theocentric piety and fidelity" and thus can continue to inform the lives of Christians.[67] Many critics, however, have charged Gustafson with having revised himself out of the Christian tradition altogether on account of his rejection of the personal God and his denial of a life after death.[68] But Gustafson points out that theology has always been engaged in revision of inherited traditions and that theological revision begins in the Bible itself.[69]

Theology in the last century has developed, modified, and criticized the agenda set for it by the Enlightenment. The major challenges have been posed by the naturalistic explanations of events offered by the modern sciences, by insights into historicism and cultural relativity, and by ethical implications of a new self-consciousness about the human character of theology as an attempt to speak about the ultimate mystery of God.

9

Conclusion

All efforts at understanding the past are motivated, to some extent, by a concern for orien-
tation in the present moment of history. Moreover,
every interpretation of history is informed,
indirectly if not directly, by a perception of the
important challenges posed by contemporary cir-
cumstances. This brief history of Christian understandings of God is intended to illuminate the
options and questions for current reflection on the
meaning of faith in God today. But the past by
itself is not sufficient to answer all the questions
and to meet every challenge of the present
moment in history. For this reason, there is no
neat and tidy conclusion to which this historical
survey leads. It points, rather, to continuing discussion, debate, and controversy as well as to an
open future as the Christian tradition continues
to develop in response to changing needs and
insights. A few general observations are in order,
however, that may serve to focus reflection.

The Christian tradition is extremely complex.
Maybe it isn't even a single tradition at all; perhaps

it is more illuminating to speak of the Christian *traditions* in the plural. There has never been a single Christian doctrine of God, just as there has never been a single doctrine of ecclesiology, Christology, or soteriology. Moreover, much that Christians have affirmed about God has been inextricably interwoven with commitments they have had with respect to these other doctrinal loci. This raises crucial questions about how we are to understand the meanings of "ecumenism" and "orthodoxy" in our time. Should Christians expect to find agreement on all the issues that have historically divided them? Or is it possible that ecumenism could be envisioned as the appreciation of the plurality within the Christian heritage? Apart from the question-begging issues of what constitutes orthodoxy and who decides it, it can be asked whether that norm—and its contrast term "heresy"—must be the only standard for evaluating what is of worth in this legacy. Furthermore, if the theological pluralism within the Bible is acknowledged, does that recognition not suggest a new way for Christians to think about the traditional sources of their theologies? The diversity of theologies in the Bible lies at the root of the great theological diversity evident in the postbiblical traditions. Hence, it doesn't make sense to ask, "Which of these traditions has correctly interpreted the Bible?" since the Bible itself is not a simple, univocal source containing a single systematic theology.

Christian doctrines of God have never been merely "Christian." Much that Christians believe is shared with Judaism and Islam. This particular overlap is explicable on the basis of their common ancestry in the tradition of ancient Israel. But Israel borrowed and adapted many features from its surrounding environment as it developed its understandings of God. Jews and Christians during the Hellenistic era found much that was attractive in Greek philosophy and assimilated this tradition into the biblical heritage. Indeed, the trinitarian doctrine of God that is most distinctive of Christianity was developed through the attempt to speak of the God of the Bible in the categories forged by the Greek philosophers. Although classical Christianity emerged at the intersection of Judaism and Hellenism, neither of these traditions was monolithic. Each harbored within itself many ways of thinking and speaking about God. A great deal of the internal plurality evident in Christianity can be explained as resulting from the various possibilities for combining diverse aspects of the one tradition with various pieces from the other. Furthermore, Christian doctrines of God were also affected by political, social, and cultural developments and did not emerge apart from very specific contexts in which the church developed its theologies. Christianity is, indeed, a complex heritage.

The crucial issue today is not only intra-Christian ecumenism but also Christianity and its relations to non-Christian religions. In our time, when the world in which we find ourselves gets smaller and increasingly interdependent, it would be wise to consider that these other religions and their histories are no less complex than Christianity. Some of these traditions speak of "God" whereas others do not use this symbol to talk about the mystery of human existence in the world. Perhaps the most important lesson Christians can learn from their own history is that there are many ways to construe the nature of ultimate reality. If Christians approach one another as well as adherents of other religious traditions with respect and humility, then perhaps something new and hopeful will emerge in the future that cannot be anticipated by merely looking to the past.

Notes

1. Judaism and the Development of Monotheism

1. The Hebrew language is written using only consonants. The name for God in the Old Testament is YHWH, which scholars believe was probably pronounced "Yahweh." At a much later stage in the development of Judaism, medieval rabbinic scribes called "Masoretes" inserted vowel points into the text of scripture to indicate how a word should be pronounced. When they came to the divine name, however, they inserted the consonants for the Hebrew word "Adonai," meaning "my Lord," since the divine name was believed too sacred to utter. Our English word "Jehovah" is the mistaken result of trying to combine the consonants for "Yahweh" and the vowels for "Adonai." In modern English translations of the Old Testament, the combination "Yahweh-Adonai" is rendered "LORD" in capital letters.

2. James A. Sanders, *Torah and Canon* (Philadelphia: Fortress Press, 1972).

2. Hellenism and the Emergence of Christianity

1. Plato, "The Apology," 26C, in *The Last Days of Socrates,* trans. Hugh Tredennick (Harmondsworth, England: Penguin Books, 1969), 56–57. See also the discussion between three Hellenistic philosophers seeking to find the mean between the extremes of "atheism" and "superstition" in Cicero's *The Nature of the Gods,* trans.

Horace C. P. McGregor (London and New York: Penguin Books, 1972).

2. In Rom. 12:1 Paul speaks of worship that is "reasonable" or "rational." The Greek word is logikè, as in the English word *logical.* Unfortunately this is usually translated as *spiritual* to make Paul sound more "churchy" and less "philosophical." Hans Dieter Betz translates this phrase as "reasonable religion" in his instructive essay, "The Foundation of Christian Ethics according to Romans 12:1-2," in *Witness and Existence: Essays in Honor of Schubert M. Ogden, ed. Philip E. Devenish and George L. Goodwin* (Chicago and London: University of Chicago Press, 1989), 61.

3. Augustine, *Confessions,* 5.14 and 6.4, trans. R. S. Pine-Coffin (Harmondsworth, England: Penguin Books, 1985), 108 and 115–16, citing 2 Cor. 3:6.

4. Gerhard von Rad, *Old Testament Theology,* trans. D. M. G. Stalker, 2 vols. (New York: Harper and Row, 1962, 1965), 2:301–8.

5. Rudolf Bultmann, *Theology of the New Testament,* trans. Kendrick Grobel, 2 vols. in one (New York: Scribner's, 1951, 1955), 1:3.

6. From Epimenides (6th century B.C.E.) and Aratus (3d century B.C.E.), respectively.

7. Betz, "The Foundation of Christian Ethics," 57–58.

8. Athenagoras, "A Plea Regarding Christians," in *Early Christian Fathers,* ed. Cyril C. Richardson (New York: Collier Books, 1970), 309.

3. The Presuppositions of the Classical Christian Tradition

1. Adolf von Harnack, *What Is Christianiity?* trans. Thomas Bailey Saunders with an Introduction by Rudolf Bultmann, Fortress Texts in Modern Theology (Philadelphia: Fortress Press, 1986), 205–9.

2. Plato, "Timaeus," 28–30B, in *Plato: The Collected Dialogues*, ed. Edith Hamilton and Huntington Cairns (Princeton: Princeton University Press, 1989), 1161–63.

3. Everett Ferguson, *Backgrounds of Early Christianity* (Grand Rapids: Eerdmans, 1993), 288–90.

4. Irenaeus, "The Refutation and Overthrow of the Knowledge Falsely So Called," in Richardson, *Early Christian Fathers*, 358–97.

5. See the insightful study by Langdon Gilkey, *Maker of Heaven and Earth: The Christian Doctrine of Creation in the Light of Modern Knowledge* (Garden City, N.Y.: Doubleday, 1959; reprint, Lanham, Md.: University Press of America, 1985).

6. Tertullian, "The Prescription against Heretics," in *Ante-Nicene Fathers*, ed. Alexander Roberts and James Donaldson (1885; reprint, Peabody, Mass.: Hendrickson Publishers, 1994), 3:246.

7. Aristotle, "Metaphysics," 12.7, in *The Basic Works of Aristotle*, ed. Richard McKeon (New York: Random House, 1941), 879–81.

8. For an excellent discussion of this issue, see Paul Tillich, *Biblical Religion and the Search for Ultimate Reality* (Chicago and London: University of Chicago Press, 1955).

9. Wolfhart Pannenberg, "The Appropriation of the Philosophical Concept of God as a Dogmatic Problem of Early Christian Theology," in *Basic Questions in Theology*, trans. George H. Kehm (Philadelphia: Fortress Press, 1971), 2:119–83.

10. "Those who lived in accordance with Reason are Christians, even though they were called godless, such as, among the Greeks, Socrates and Heraclitus and others like them. . . ." Justin Martyr, "First Apology," in Richardson, *Early Christian Fathers*, 272.

4. Christology and the Doctrine of the Trinity

1. "The Nicene Creed" refers both to the original "Creed of Nicea" (325) and the official version later promulgated at the Council of Constantinople called "The Constantinopolitan Creed" (381). Both are conveniently found in John H. Leith, *Creeds of the Church*, 3d ed. (Louisville: John Knox Press, 1982), 28–33.

2. Athanasius, *On the Incarnation*, with an Introduction by C. S. Lewis (Crestwood, N.Y.: St. Vladimir's Orthodox Theological Seminary, 1982), 26.

3. Jaroslav Pelikan comments: "It is very significant that Christian theologians customarily set down the doctrine of the impassibility of God as an axiom, without bothering to provide very much biblical support or theological proof." *The Emergence of the Catholic Tradition (100–600)*, vol. 1 of *The Christian Tradition: A History of the Development of Doctrine* (Chicago and London: University of Chicago Press, 1971), 52.

4. J. N. D. Kelly, *Early Christian Doctrines*, revised ed. (San Francisco: Harper and Row, 1978), 115.

5. Ibid., 128.

6. Augustine, "The Trinity," in *Augustine: Later Works*, ed. John Burnaby, Library of Christian Classics: Ichthus Edition (Philadelphia: Westminster Press, 1955), 54–55, 88

7. Gregory of Nyssa, "Concerning What We Should Think of Saying That There Are Not Three Gods *to Ablabius*," in *The Trinitarian Controversy*, ed. and trans. William G. Rusch (Philadelphia: Fortress Press, 1980), 152.

8. "Thus you should learn that unbegotten and God are not the same." Gregory of Nazianzus, "Third Theological Oration concerning the Son," in *The Trinitarian Controversy*, 139.

9. Christopher Morse, *Not Every Spirit: A Dogmatics of Christian Disbelief* (Valley Forge, Pa.: Trinity Press International, 1994), 174–76, 184–89.

5. The Middle Ages

1. Augustine, "The Soliloquies," in *Augustine: Earlier Writings*, trans. John H. S. Burleigh, Library of Christian Classics (Philadelphia: Westminster Press, 1953), 17–18, 23–63.

2. Peter Brown, *Augustine of Hippo* (Berkeley and Los Angeles: University of California Press, 1969), 85.

3. *Confessions*, 1.1.

4. Augustine, *On Christian Doctrine*, trans. D. W. Robertson Jr., Library of Liberal Arts (Saddle River, N.J.: Prentice Hall, 1958), 9–10, 30–33.

5. *Confessions*, 7.12–13, pp. 148–49.

6. Augustine, *City of God*, 11.6, trans. Henry Bettenson (Harmondsworth, Eng. and New York: Penguin Books, 1972), 436.

7. *On Christian Doctrine*, 31–33.

8. *City of God*, 14.28, p. 593.

9. Augustine, "The Spirit and the Letter," in *Later Works*, 193–250.

10. Pseudo-Dionysius, "The Divine Names," in *The Complete Works*, trans. Colm Luibheid with foreword, notes, and translation collaboration by Paul Rorem, Classics of Western Spirituality (New York: Paulist Press, 1987), 50.

11. According to Bultmann, Paul uses the language of Stoic pantheism in two places: Rom. 11:36 and 1 Cor. 8:4-6. Bultmann also comments: "The Hellenistic manner of describing the nature of God by the *via negationis* (the way of negation) is quickly appropriated by Christian language in its use of adjectives formed with the alpha-privative prefix." Examples are "invisible" (Rom. 1:20) and "incorruptible" (Rom. 1:23). *Theology of the New Testament*, 1:72.

12. St. John of Damascus, *On the Divine Images*, trans. David Anderson (Crestwood, N.Y.: St. Vladimir's Seminary Press, 1997), 19, 23–24.

13. Anselm, "An Address (*Proslogion*)," in *A Scholastic Miscellany: Anselm to Ockham*, ed. Eugene R. Fairweather, Library of Christian Classics: Ichthus Edition (Philadelphia: Westminster Press, 1956), 73.

14. Ibid., 76–81.

15. Ibid., 86.

16. Ibid., 86–87.

17. Anselm, "Why God Became Man," in *A Scholastic Miscellany*, 100.

18. "An Address (*Proslogion*)," 73–75. Cf. Immanuel Kant, *Critique of Pure Reason*, trans. Norman Kemp Smith (New York: St. Martin's Press, 1965), 500–507;

and Charles Hartshorne, *Anselm's Discovery: A Re-Examination of the Ontological Proof for God's Existence* (Lasalle, Ill.: Open Court Publishing, 1965).

19. Thomas Aquinas, *Summa Theologiae*, I, q. 2, art. 1, in *Aquinas on Nature and Grace*, trans. A. M. Fairweather, Library of Christian Classics: Ichthus Edition (Philadelphia: Westminster Press, 1954), 51.

20. Ibid., I, q. 2, art. 2, pp. 52–53.

21. Ibid., I, q. 2, art. 3, pp. 53–56.

22. Ibid., I, q. 1, art. 1, pp. 35–37.

23. Ibid., I, q. 1, art. 8, p. 46.

24. Ibid., I, q. 3, art. 2, p. 60; cf. Aristotle, "Metaphysics," 12. 7, in *The Basic Works of Aristotle*, pp. 879–81.

25. St. Thomas Aquinas, *Summa Theologica*, I. q. 46, art. 2, translated by the Fathers of the English Dominican Province, complete English ed. in 5 vols. (Westminster, Md.: Christian Classics, 1981), 1:242–44.

26. *Summa Theologiae*, I, q. 1, art. 10, in *Nature and Grace*, pp. 48–49.

27. *Summa Theologica*, I, q. 13, art. 3, p. 62.

6. The Protestant Reformation

1. Julian of Norwich, *Showings*, trans. Edmund Colledge, O.S.A., and James Walsh, S.J., Classics of Western Spirituality (New York: Paulist Press, 1978), 135.

2. Ibid., 149, 196.

3. Ibid., 267–69.

4. Ibid., 298–99.

5. Ibid., 300–301.

6. Ibid., 285.

7. *Summa Theologiae*, 1–2ae, q. 114, art. 3 and 1–2ae, q. 114, art. 6, in *Nature and Grace*, pp. 206–8 and 211–12.

8. Martin Luther, *Lectures on Romans*, ed. Wilhelm Pauck, Library of Christian Classics (Philadelphia: Westminster Press, 1961), 18.

9. Martin Luther, "The Freedom of the Christian," in *Three Treatises*, from the American ed. of *Luther's*

Works (Philadelphia: Fortress Press, 1970), 277–316.

10. Luther wrote: "The sacraments . . . are not fulfilled when they are taking place, but when they are being believed." "The Babylonian Captivity of the Church," in *Three Treatises*, 189.

11. Paul Althaus says that, for Luther, "The God of the Bible is not unequivocally the God of the gospel. The God of the Bible is not only the God of all grace but is also the God who, if he wills, hardens and rejects. . . . The God revealed and preached in the gospel must be distinguished from the hidden God who is not preached, the God who works all things." *The Theology of Martin Luther*, trans. Robert C. Schultz (Philadelphia: Fortress Press, 1966), 276. See the very illuminating essay by B. A. Gerrish, "'To the Unknown God': Luther and Calvin on the Hiddenness of God," in *The Old Protestantism and the New: Essays on the Reformation Heritage* (Edinburgh: T. & T. Clark, 1982), 131–49.

12. John Calvin, *Institutes of the Christian Religion*, trans. Ford Lewis Battles, ed. John T. McNeill, 2 vols., Library of Christian Classics (Philadelphia: Westminster Press, 1960), 2.7.12 (1:360), cited according to book, chapter, and paragraph with page references to the McNeill edition in parentheses.

13. *Inst.*, 2.14.1–2 (1:482–44); cf. *Inst.*, 2.13.4 (1:481).

14. Ibid., 1.2.1 (1:41).

15. B. A. Gerrish, *Grace and Gratitude: The Eucharistic Theology of John Calvin* (Minneapolis: Fortress Press, 1993), 41–48; see also his essay "The Mirror of God's Goodness: A Key Metaphor in Calvin's View of Man," in *The Old Protestantism and the New*, 150–59.

16. *Inst.*, 1.3.1 (1:43–44).

17. "Letter to Sadoleto," in John Calvin and Jacopo Sadoleto, *A Reformation Debate*, ed. John C. Olin (Grand Rapids, Mich.: Baker Book House, 1966), 58.

18. *Inst.*, 1.1.1 (1:35).

19. Ibid., 1.2.1 (1:40).

20. Ibid., 1.13.1 (1:121); 1.6.1 (1:70).

21. This nonpersonal image is of Platonic prove-

nance. Calvin agreed with Plato that the reason God made the universe was on account of his goodness. *Inst.*, 1.5.6 (1:59); cf. Plato, "Timaeus," 29D–30A, in *The Collected Dialogues*, 1162. See Gerrish, *Grace and Gratitude*, 31–41. Calvin's favorite personal metaphor for God is "father," but Jane Dempsey Douglas has pointed out that Calvin also availed himself of the metaphor of "mother" to talk about God. "Calvin's Use of Metaphorical Language for God: God as Enemy and God as Mother," in *Archive for Reformation History* 77 (1986):126–40.

22. *Inst.*, 1.16.1 (1:197).

23. Ibid., 1.16.1 (1:197–98).

24. Ibid., 1.16.4 (1:202), 1.16.3 (1:200).

25. Ibid., 1.17.11 (1:224).

26. Ibid., 1.16.3 (1:200–201).

27. Ibid., 1.17.6 (1: 218).

28. Ibid., 1.16.8 (1:207).

29. Ibid., 1.5.5 (1:58); I have adapted Battles's translation to bring it into greater conformity with the Latin text. *Institutio christianae religionis* (1559), vols. 3–5, in *Ioannis Calvini opera selecta*, ed. Peter Barth, Wilhelm Niesel, and Dora Scheuner, 5 vols. (Munich: Christian Kaiser Verlag, 1926–52), 3:50.

30. Karl Barth spoke of "the strangely unemphatic and 'loveless' position that the doctrine of the Trinity occupies in the *Institutes*" and suggested that "had Caroli been more acute he would have had to accuse Calvin and his party of Sabellianism rather than Arianism." Karl Barth, *The Theology of John Calvin*, trans. Geoffey W. Bromiley (Grand Rapids, Mich.: Eerdmans, 1995), 312, 327.

31. B. A. Gerrish, "Theology within the Limits of Piety Alone: Schleiermacher and Calvin's Notion of God," in *The Old Protestantism and the New*, 196–207.

32. *Inst.*, 1.13.3 (1:124).

33. Ibid., 1.14.4 (1:164).

34. Ibid., 1.15.4 (1:190).

35. Ibid., 1.2.2 (1:41–42).

36. Ibid., 1.2.1 (1:39).

37. Barth, *Theology of John Calvin*, 326.

38. John Wesley, "Predestination Calmly Considered," in *John Wesley*, ed. Albert C. Outler (New York: Oxford University Press, 1964), 427–72.

7. The Enlightenment and the Modern Era

1. James C. Livingston, *Modern Christian Thought*, 2d ed., 2 vols. (Upper Saddle River, N.J.: Prentice-Hall, 1997), 1:15–16.

2. John Locke, *A Letter Concerning Toleration*, Great Books in Philosophy (Amherst, N.Y.: Prometheus Books, 1990).

3. Thomas Aquinas, *Summa Theologiae*, I, q. 2, art. 2, in *Nature and Grace*, 52.

4. David Hume, *Dialogues Concerning Natural Religion*, ed. Henry D. Aiken, Hafner Library of Classics (New York and London: Hafner Press, 1948).

5. David Hume, *The Natural History of Religion*, ed. H. E. Root, Library of Modern Religious Thought (Stanford, Calif.: Stanford University Press, 1956).

6. David Hume, "Of Miracles," in *An Inquiry Concerning Human Understanding* (New York, 1955), 123, cited by Livingston, *Modern Christian Thought*, 1:51.

7. Kant, *Critique of Pure Reason*, 550–51.

8. Immanuel Kant, *Critique of Practical Reason*, trans. Mary Gregor, Cambridge Texts in the History of Philosophy (Cambridge: Cambridge University Press, 1997), 110–11.

9. Immanuel Kant, *Religion within the Limits of Reason Alone*, trans. Theodore M. Greene and Hoyt H. Hudson (New York: Harper Torchbooks, 1960).

10. *Critique of Pure Reason*, 29.

11. Paul Tillich, *A History of Christian Thought: From Its Judaic and Hellenistic Origins to Existentialism*, ed. Carl E. Braaten (New York: Touchstone Books, 1967, 1968), 361. Tillich explains that he first heard this "oversimplification" in a lecture by Julius Kaftan (1848–1926).

12. Friedrich Schleiermacher, *On Religion: Speeches to Its Cultured Despisers*, trans. Richard Crouter, 2d ed.,

Cambridge Texts in the History of Philosophy (Cambridge: Cambridge University Press, 1996), 23.

13. Benedict de Spinoza, "A Theologico-Political Treatise," in *A Theologico-Political Treatise and A Political Treatise*, trans. R. H. M. Elwes (New York: Dover Publications, 1951), 120–32.

14. Hume, *Dialogues Concerning Natural Religion*, 42.

15. Benedict de Spinoza, "The Ethics," in *On the Improvement of the Understanding, The Ethics, and Correspondence*, trans. R. H. M. Elwes (New York: Dover Publications, 1955), 68–69.

16. Schleiermacher, *Speeches*, 25.

17. See the excellent study by Julia A. Lamm, *The Living God: Schleiermacher's Theological Appropriation of Spinoza* (University Park, Pa.: Pennsylvania State University Press, 1996).

18. Friedrich Schleiermacher, *The Christian Faith*, ed. H. R. Mackintosh and J. S. Stewart (Philadelphia: Fortress Press, 1976), ¶4, p. 12.

19. *The Christian Faith*, ¶47, p. 178.

20. *Speeches*, 49.

21. *The Christian Faith*, ¶51.1, pp. 200–202.

22. Friedrich Schleiermacher, *On the Glaubenslehre: Two Letters to Dr. Lücke*, trans. James Duke and Francis Fiorenza, American Academy of Religion Texts and Translations Series (Chico, Calif.: Scholars Press, 1981), 64.

23. *The Christian Faith*, ¶7–11, pp. 31–60.

24. Ibid., ¶94, p. 385.

25. Ibid., ¶15, pp. 76–78, ¶ 26, pp. 111–12.

26. Ibid., ¶10, "Postscript," p. 52.

27. Unfortunately, in our time the word *dogmatic* has taken on the connotation of "authoritarian" or "doctrinaire." This is not the meaning of the term in the classical Christian tradition, where it means simply the systematic elucidation of the church's teachings, that is, its doctrines or dogmas.

28. *The Christian Faith*, ¶50, p. 194.

29. Ibid., ¶172.1, p. 748.

30. Ibid., ¶170.3, p. 741.

31. G. W. F. Hegel, *Phenomenology of Spirit*, in *G. W. F. Hegel: Theologian of the Spirit*, ed. Peter C. Hodgson, Making of Modern Theology: Nineteenth and Twentieth-Century Texts (Minneapolis: Fortress Press, 1997), 93.

32. Hegel, *Early Theological Writings*, in *Theologian of the Spirit*, 65.

33. Peter C. Hodgson, "Introduction," in *Theologian of the Spirit*, 27. Hodgson's essay is an excellent overview of Hegel's achievement and its enduring significance.

34. Ludwig Feuerbach, *The Essence of Christianity*, trans. George Eliot (New York: Harper Torchbooks, 1957), 14, 153.

35. Ibid., 53.

36. Karl Marx and Friedrich Engels, *The Communist Manifesto*, trans. Samuel Moore (New York: Bantam Books, 1992), 40.

37. Ibid., 30.

38. A very good account of Darwin for the nonspecialist is found in Loren Eisley, *Darwin's Century: Evolution and the Men Who Discovered It* (Garden City, N.Y.: Anchor Books, 1961).

39. Sigmund Freud, *The Future of an Illusion*, trans. James Strachey (New York: W. W. Norton, 1961).

40. Ernst Troeltsch, "The Dogmatics of the History-of-Religions School," in *Religion in History*, trans. James Luther Adams and Walter F. Bense, Fortress Texts in Modern Theology (Minneapolis: Fortress Press, 1991), 87–108.

41. Friedrich Nietzsche, "The Madman," cited by Walter A. Kaufmann, *Nietzsche: Philosopher, Psychologist, Antichrist* (Princeton: Princeton University Press, 1950), 74–75.

8. The Twentieth Century

1. Karl Barth, "The Revelation of God as the Abolition of Religion," in *Church Dogmatics*, 1.2, ed. G. W. Bromiley and T. F. Torrance (Edinburgh: T. & T. Clark, 1956), §17, pp. 280–361.

2. Karl Barth and Emil Brunner, *Natural Theology, Comprising "Nature and Grace" by Professor Emil Brunner and the reply "No" by Dr. Karl Barth*, trans. Peter Fraenkel (London: Geoffrey Blis [Centenary Press], 1946).

3. Barth, "The Word of God and the Task of the Ministry," in *The Word of God and the Word of Man*, trans. Douglas Horton (1928; reprint, Gloucester, Mass.: Peter Smith, 1978), 196.

4. Barth, *Church Dogmatics*, 3.2 (Edinburgh: T. & T. Clark, 1960), 609.

5. Ibid., 1.1 (Edinburgh: T. & T. Clark, 1936), §8, p. 295.

6. Ibid., 2.1 (Edinburgh: T. & T. Clark, 1957), §28, p. 257.

7. Barth, *The Humanity of God* (Atlanta: John Knox Press, 1982), 49.

8. Paul Tillich, *Dynamics of Faith* (New York: Harper Torchbooks, 1957), 1.

9. Tillich, *Systematic Theology*, 3 vols. in one (Chicago: University of Chicago Press, 1951, 1957, 1963), 3:130.

10. *The Book of Concord: The Confessions of the Evangelical Lutheran Church*, trans. and ed. Theodore G. Tappert in collaboration with Jaroslav Pelikan, Robert H. Fischer, and Arthur C. Piepkorn (Philadelphia: Fortress Press, 1959), 365.

11. Tillich, *Systematic Theology*, 1:235.

12. Initially Tillich held to the view that the one non-symbolic statement about God we can make is that "God is being-itself." He later modified this and said that the only nonsymbolic thing we can say is that all our language about God is symbolic. But this is not properly a statement about God, only a statement about our language for God. See *Systematic Theology*, 1:238 and 2:9.

13. Tillich, *Biblical Religion and the Search for Ultimate Reality*, 83.

14. Tillich, *A History of Christian Thought*, 408.

15. *Systematic Theology*, 1:6-8.

16. Tillich, *The Courage to Be* (New Haven and London: Yale University Press, 1952), 174.

17. Idem, *Dynamics of Faith*, 45.

18. Idem, *The Courage to Be*, 189–90.

19. H. Richard Niebuhr, *Radical Monotheism and Western Culture with Supplementary Essays* (New York: Harper Torchbooks, 1960), 11, 23.

20. H. Richard Niebuhr, *The Meaning of Revelation* (New York: Macmillan, 1941), 57.

21. Idem, *Radical Monotheism and Western Culture*, 32.

22. Ibid., 38, 34.

23. Ibid., 56.

24. Ibid., 42.

25. H. Richard Niebuhr, "The Doctrine of the Trinity and the Unity of the Church," in *H. Richard Niebuhr: Theology, History, and Culture*, ed. William Stacy Johnson (New Haven and London: Yale University Press, 1996), 52. See also the good essay by Douglas F. Ottati, "The Sense the Trinity Makes," in *Hopeful Realism: Reclaiming the Poetry of Theology* (Cleveland: Pilgrim Press, 1999), 39–50.

26. Charles Hartshorne, *The Divine Relativity: A Social Conception of God* (New Haven and London: Yale University Press, 1948).

27. Alfred North Whitehead, *Process and Reality*, corrected ed., ed. David Ray Griffin and Donald W. Sherburne (New York and London: Free Press, 1978), 349.

28. Ibid., 342.

29. Daniel Day Williams, *The Spirit and the Forms of Love* (New York: Harper and Row, 1968).

30. Schubert M. Ogden, "The Reality of God," in *The Reality of God and Other Essays* (New York: Harper and Row, 1977), 1–70.

31. John B. Cobb Jr., *A Christian Natural Theology based on the Thought of Alfred North Whitehead* (Philadelphia: Westminster Press, 1965), 252–84; see also Cobb's *Living Options in Protestant Theology: A Survey of Methods* (Philadelphia: Westminster Press, 1962; reprint, Lanham, Md.: University Press of America, 1986), 312–23.

32. Gustavo Gutiérez, *A Theology of Liberation*, 15th Anniversary ed., trans. Sister Caridad Inda and John Eagleson (Maryknoll, N.Y.: Orbis Books, 1988), 111.

33. James H. Cone, "Preface to the 1997 Edition," in *God of the Oppressed*, revised edition (Maryknoll, N.Y.: Orbis Books, 1997), xi.

34. Ibid., xiii–xiv.

35. Ibid., 3.

36. Mary Daly, *Beyond God the Father: Toward a Philosophy of Women's Liberation* (Boston: Beacon Press, 1985), 19. Already in 1951 Paul Tillich wrote: "The criticism by psychology and sociology of personalistic symbols for man's relation to God must be taken seriously by theologians. It must be acknowledged that the two central symbols, Lord and Father, are stumbling blocks for many people because theologians and preachers have been unwilling to listen to the often shocking insights into psychological consequences of the traditional use of these symbols." *Systematic Theology*, 1:288.

37. Sallie McFague, *Models of God: Theology for an Ecological, Nuclear Age* (Philadelphia: Fortress Press, 1987), 69–180.

38. For a very good example of a feminist retrieval and reshaping of classical trinitarian doctrine, see Elizabeth A. Johnson, *She Who Is: The Mystery of God in Feminist Theological Discourse* (New York: Crossroad, 1996). For a related treatment, see Catherine Mowry LaCugna, *God for Us: The Trinity and Christian Life* (San Francisco: HarperCollins, 1991).

39. For a discussion of the issues involved on both sides, see Ted Peters, *God as Trinity: Relationality and Temporality in Divine Life* (Louisville: Westminster John Knox Press, 1993), 46–55. It is noteworthy that Luther did not insist upon the trinitarian formula at baptism. "The Babylonian Captivity of the Church," in *Three Treatises*, 185–86.

40. Daphne Hampson, *After Christianity* (Valley Forge, Pa.: Trinity Press International, 1996).

41. Karl Rahner, *Foundations of Christian Faith: An Introduction to the Idea of Christianity*, trans. William V. Dych (New York: Crossroad, 1986), 136–37.

42. Barth, *Church Dogmatics* 1.1, p. 355; Rahner, *Foundations of Christian Faith*, 136–37.

43. Jürgen Moltmann, *The Trinity and the Kingdom: The Doctrine of God*, trans. Margaret Kohl (Minneapolis: Fortress Press, 1993), 140.

44. Ibid., 131.

45. See ibid., 129–50, for his "Criticism of Christian Monotheism," where he criticizes Barth and Rahner, and also 243, n. 43, for his repudiation of the charge of tritheism: "As the history of theology shows, there has never been a Christian tritheist. Even Barth does not name any, although he argues so vigorously against tritheism. The standard argument against 'tritheism' practically serves everywhere to disguise the writer's own modalism." Whereas Moltmann refuses to allow his rejection of monotheism in favor of trinitarianism to be branded as tritheistic, at least one theologian who is sympathetic to his argument has no hesitation in applying the label. Shirley C. Guthrie suggests that "perhaps it is worth running the risk of being called tritheistic . . . if we thought of Christian faith not as one among other monotheistic religions." *Christian Doctrine*, revised edition (Louisville: Westminster John Knox Press, 1994), 93–94.

46. Moltmann, *The Trinity and the Kingdom*, 174–75.

47. Ibid., 24.

48. Ibid., 25

49. Gordon D. Kaufman, *In Face of Mystery: A Constructive Theology* (Cambridge, Mass.: Harvard University Press, 1993), 369.

50. Ibid., 451.

51. Ibid., 237.

52. See his illuminating autobiographical reflections in "My Life and My Theological Reflection: Two Central Themes," in *American Journal of Theology and Philosophy* 22 (January 2001): 3–32.

53. *In Face of Mystery*, 271.

54. Kaufman acknowledges his debt to Henry Nelson Wieman's *The Source of Human Good* (Chicago: University of Chicago Press, 1946). Wieman also developed a notion of God as "creativity" or "the creative process." See Kaufman's "My Life and My Theological Reflection," 27.

55. Kaufman, *In Face of Mystery*, 317.

56. Ibid., xv.

57. Ibid., 439.

58. James M. Gustafson, *Ethics from a Theocentric Perspective*, 2 vols. (Chicago: University of Chicago Press, 1981, 1984), 1:140, 158. Gustafson is modifying a view of theology proposed by Julian N. Hartt, who described it as "an intention to relate to all things in ways appropriate to their belonging to God." Hartt, "Encounter and Inference in Our Awareness of God," in *The God Experience*, ed. Joseph P. Whelan, S.J. (New York: Newman Press, 1971), 52.

59. *Ethics from a Theocentric Perspective*, 1:88, 190.

60. Ibid., 1:157.

61. Ibid., 1:37–48.

62. Gustafson says, "Barth says vividly and categorically: 'God is for man.' I do not say God is against man. But the sense in which God is for man must be spelled out in a carefully qualified way." Ibid., 1:181.

63. For Gustafson's detailed account of his continuities and discontinuities with the Reformed tradition, see his chapter entitled "A Preference for the Reformed Tradition," in Ibid., 1:157–93.

64. Ibid., 1:251, citing *Inst.* 1.5.5 (1:58).

65. Ibid., 1:264.

66. Ibid., 1:327.

67. Ibid., 1:276.

68. For some of the critical (as well as appreciative) responses, see *James M. Gustafson's Theocentric Ethics: Interpretations and Assessments*, ed. Harlan R. Beckley and Charles M. Swezey (Macon, Ga.: Mercer University Press, 1988).

69. *Ethics from a Theocentric Perspective*, 1:136–50.

For Further Reading

Karen Armstrong, *A History of God: The 4,000-Year Quest of Judaism, Christianity, and Islam* (New York: Knopf, 1993).

Marcus J. Borg, *The God We Never Knew: Beyond Dogmatic Religion to a More Authentic Contemporary Faith* (San Francisco: HarperCollins, 1997).

Philip Clayton, *The Problem of Evil in Modern Thought* (Grand Rapids, Mich.: Eerdmans, 2000).

Langdon Gilkey, "God" in *Christian Theology: An Introduction to Its Traditions and Tasks*, ed. Peter C. Hodgson and Robert H. King, newly updated edition (Minneapolis: Fortress Press, 1994): 88–113.

Sallie McFague, *Models of God: Theology for an Ecological, Nuclear Age* (Philadelphia: Fortress Press, 1987).

Schubert M. Ogden, *The Reality of God and Other Essays* (San Francisco: Harper and Row, 1977).

Francis Schüssler Fiorenza and Gordon D. Kaufman, "God" in *Critical Terms for Religious Studies*, ed. Mark C. Taylor (Chicago and London: The University of Chicago Press, 1998): 136–59.

Acknowledgments

An earlier draft of this essay was written for the
"Workgroup in Constructive Theology," which
meets every spring at Vanderbilt Divinity School.
I have benefited from the criticisms and suggestions for improvement given by my friends and
colleagues in that group, even though I have failed
to do justice to all their good ideas in this final
version of the essay. I especially wish to thank
my fellow members of the subgroup on the
doctrine of God for the numerous discussions over
the past few years that have pushed me toward
greater clarity in my thinking on this topic:
Laurel Schneider, Ellen Armour, Don Compier,
Paul DeHart, Francis Schüssler Fiorenza, and
Peter C. Hodgson.

A special word of thanks goes to Michael West
at Fortress Press who, to my surprise and delight,
initiated the project of this book with his proposal
that I revise the essay into a short volume. Zan
Ceeley and Bob Todd, also of Fortress Press,
deserve mention for their assistance on my behalf
in preparation for the book's publication.

At United Theological Seminary, I received assistance from a number of persons: Mary Ann Nelson, my faithful and diligent secretary for the past eleven years, helped me with typing; our reference librarian, Dale Dobias, came to my assistance on many occasions; my good faculty colleagues, Carolyn J. Pressler, Rosetta E. Ross, Richard Weis, and Tatha Wiley, shared their expertise or gave needed encouragement at crucial moments; Matthew Bersagel Braley, Vicki Gaylord, Todd Smith Lippert, James R. Wilson, and Christi Wirth-Davis—five excellent students—helped me more than they know through their tough questions and honest feedback.

I am also very grateful to the Institute for Reformed Theology at Union Theological Seminary—Presbyterian School of Christian Education in Richmond, Virginia, for inviting me to participate in a colloquy on "The Divine Activity in Recent Theology" during the academic year 2000–2001. The colloquy, which was ably led by Douglas F. Ottati, gave me an extended opportunity to ponder many matters here addressed in the company of an engaging group of pastors, students, and professors.

One theologian whose work was carefully studied during the course of the colloquy was James M. Gustafson. I wish to thank Professor Gustafson for his generosity and patience in allowing me to engage him in lengthy correspondence and long hours of conversation about his own "theocentric" perspective. His writings have challenged me to rethink many of my previous assumptions about God as well as to search for a more adequate theological articulation of my deepest religious convictions.

During the process of revising the essay for publication I have had occasion to remember my deceased father who could never understand the doctrine of the Trinity. He availed himself of every opportunity to ask a minister to explain it to him. In my teaching of seminarians I try to impress upon them the importance of taking the historical study of theology seriously since there will always be persons like my father in the congregations to which they will be called to serve as interpreters of the Christian tradition. It is for such inquiring persons in the churches that my little book is intended.

I dedicate this work to my uncle and aunt, George and Harriet Capetz, who not only exemplify the virtues of faith, hope, and love but also provide me with a rock of stability in my life. In a time when there has been much contentious public debate about "family values," they have shown me in a very personal way what the word "family" truly means. I give thanks to God for them every day.